Title: Mastering Time: Strategies for Effective Work in the AI Era

Chapter I: AI in Our Lives Today

I. Exploring the impact of AI on daily life
II. A brief history of artificial intelligence
III. Types of AI: Narrow AI, General AI, and Super AI

Chapter II: How AI Works

I. Data as the foundation of AI
II. Machine Learning and Deep Learning explained
III. Neural networks: The building blocks of AI systems

Chapter III: Future Trends in AI

I. The breakthroughs shaping tomorrow
II. Key industries disrupted by AI advancements

Chapter IV: AI in the Workplace

I. Streamlining workflows with AI automation
II. Tools like ChatGPT, Notion AI, and their applications

Chapter V: AI and Creativity

I. AI in writing, art, and music
II. Leveraging AI to enhance creative processes

Chapter VI: AI in Education

I. Personalized learning with AI tools
II. Transforming education systems through AI integration

Chapter VII: AI for Business Growth

I. Optimizing operations with AI-driven solutions
II. Revolutionizing marketing with personalization and analytics

Chapter VIII: Launching an AI-Powered Business

I. Profitable ideas for AI-based startups
II. Finding resources and building partnerships

Chapter IX: Managing AI in Organizations

I. Preparing teams for AI adoption
II. Navigating challenges and mitigating risks

Chapter X: AI in Healthcare

I. AI-powered diagnostics and medical research
II. The role of AI in transforming patient care

Chapter XI: AI and Smart Living

I. Smart homes, autonomous vehicles, and beyond
II. AI's environmental implications

Chapter XII: Ethics and Challenges of AI

I. Privacy, data security, and ethical concerns
II. Balancing human roles with AI capabilities

Chapter XIII: Learning AI

I. A roadmap for beginners
II. Recommended platforms and tools for mastering AI

Chapter XIV: Using AI in Everyday Life

I. Communicating effectively with AI tools
II. Enhancing productivity through AI

Chapter XV: Thriving in the AI Era

I. Preparing your mindset for an AI-driven future
II. Human skills that remain irreplaceable

Chapter I: AI in Our Lives Today
I. Exploring the impact of AI on daily life

Artificial Intelligence (AI) has seamlessly integrated into many aspects of our daily lives, transforming how we work, communicate, and make decisions. Here are some key areas where AI is making a significant impact:

1. Communication and Personal Assistance

- **Virtual Assistants**: Tools like Siri, Alexa, and Google Assistant use natural language processing (NLP) to perform tasks such as setting reminders, answering queries, or controlling smart home devices.
- **Chatbots**: Many customer service interactions are now handled by AI-driven chatbots, which provide instant responses and resolve common issues.

2. Healthcare

- **Diagnostics and Treatment**: AI helps in diagnosing diseases by analyzing medical data and imaging, enabling earlier detection and personalized treatment plans.
- **Fitness and Health Monitoring**: Wearables like Fitbit and smartwatches use AI to monitor physical activity, heart rates, and sleep patterns, encouraging healthier lifestyles.

3. Transportation

- **Navigation**: Applications like Google Maps use AI to provide real-time traffic updates and optimize routes.

- **Autonomous Vehicles**: Companies like Tesla are pioneering self-driving cars, which rely on AI to interpret surroundings and make driving decisions.

4. Entertainment

- **Streaming Services**: Platforms like Netflix and Spotify use AI algorithms to recommend content based on user preferences and viewing/listening history.
- **Gaming**: AI enhances gaming experiences through smarter non-playable characters (NPCs) and adaptive difficulty levels.

5. Retail and Shopping

- **Personalized Recommendations**: Online retailers like Amazon use AI to suggest products tailored to individual preferences.
- **Inventory Management**: AI optimizes stock levels and supply chain logistics, ensuring items are available when needed.

6. Work and Productivity

- **Automation**: AI automates repetitive tasks, enabling professionals to focus on creative or strategic activities.
- **Collaboration Tools**: Platforms like Microsoft Teams and Slack integrate AI to transcribe meetings, suggest responses, and streamline workflows.

7. Education

- **Personalized Learning**: AI-powered platforms like Khan Academy and Duolingo adapt to individual learning paces and styles.
- **Accessibility**: AI tools provide real-time transcription and translation, making education more inclusive.

8. Smart Homes

- **Energy Efficiency**: Smart thermostats like Nest use AI to learn user preferences and optimize energy usage.
- **Security**: AI enhances home security through facial recognition and anomaly detection in camera feeds.

9. Social Media

- **Content Moderation**: AI helps filter harmful or inappropriate content.
- **Personalized Feeds**: Algorithms prioritize content that aligns with user interests, increasing engagement.

10. Finance and Banking

- **Fraud Detection**: AI identifies unusual transactions to prevent fraud.
- **Financial Planning**: Apps like Mint and robo-advisors use AI to offer tailored financial advice and investment strategies.

II. A brief history of artificial intelligence

The field of artificial intelligence has a rich history that spans decades, with milestones marking its evolution from an abstract concept to a transformative force in technology. Below is an overview of the key developments in AI:

1. Early Concepts and Foundations

- **Ancient Ideas**: The idea of intelligent machines dates back to myths and stories like the Greek myth of Talos or the concept of automata in various cultures.
- **Philosophical Foundations**: Thinkers such as René Descartes and Alan Turing explored the nature of human intelligence and whether machines could emulate it. Turing's 1950 paper, *"Computing Machinery and Intelligence,"* introduced the **Turing Test** as a way to evaluate machine intelligence.

2. Birth of AI (1950s)

- **The Dartmouth Workshop (1956)**: Regarded as the "birth of AI," this event brought together pioneers like John McCarthy, Marvin Minsky, Nathaniel Rochester, and Claude Shannon to define the field of artificial intelligence.
- **Early Programs**: Programs like the Logic Theorist (1956) by Allen Newell and Herbert A. Simon were among the first to mimic human reasoning, solving mathematical problems.

3. Golden Age of AI (1950s–1970s)

- **Expert Systems**: AI research focused on creating systems that could mimic expert human decision-making in specific domains.
- **Advances in Problem-Solving**: AI programs like ELIZA (an early chatbot) and SHRDLU (a natural language understanding system) demonstrated the potential for machine-human interaction.
- **Limitations Exposed**: Researchers soon realized the limitations of early AI, particularly in handling real-world complexity and ambiguity.

4. AI Winter (1970s–1980s)

- **Reduced Funding**: Unrealistic expectations and slow progress led to a decline in funding and interest in AI research, a period referred to as the **AI Winter.**
- **Technical Barriers**: The lack of computational power and inadequate data hindered the development of AI systems.

5. Renewed Interest and Machine Learning (1980s–1990s)

- **Neural Networks Revival**: The re-emergence of interest in **artificial neural networks**, inspired by biological brains, provided a new direction for AI.
- **Expert Systems in Business**: AI applications found success in industries like finance, healthcare, and manufacturing.

6. The Era of Data and Deep Learning (2000s–2010s)

- **Big Data**: The rise of the internet and digital transformation provided vast amounts of data, essential for training AI models.
- **Deep Learning**: Algorithms like convolutional neural networks (CNNs) and recurrent neural networks (RNNs) achieved breakthroughs in areas such as image and speech recognition.
- **AI in Everyday Applications**: Technologies like IBM's Watson winning *Jeopardy!* (2011) and the introduction of virtual assistants like Siri marked AI's growing presence in daily life.

7. Modern AI (2010s–Present)

- **Natural Language Processing (NLP)**: Advances in NLP, particularly with models like GPT and BERT, enabled sophisticated text generation, translation, and comprehension.
- **Reinforcement Learning**: Techniques such as those used in AlphaGo (2016) and OpenAI's Dota 2 bots
- **Ethics and Regulation**: The rapid development of AI prompted discussions around ethical use, privacy concerns, and regulation to ensure responsible deployment.

8. Future Prospects

- As AI continues to advance, emerging fields like general AI, quantum AI, and neuromorphic computing may redefine the boundaries of what machines can achieve.

III. Types of AI: Narrow AI, General AI, and Super AI

Artificial Intelligence is categorized based on its capabilities and scope of operation. The three primary types are **Narrow AI**, **General AI**, and **Super AI**. Each represents a different level of advancement and functionality.

1. Narrow AI (Weak AI)

- **Definition**: Narrow AI refers to systems designed to perform specific tasks with a high degree of efficiency. These AI systems do not possess general intelligence or understanding beyond their programmed domain.
- **Characteristics**:
  - Focused on a single task or a set of closely related tasks.
  - Operates under predefined parameters and lacks the ability to perform outside its scope.
  - Relies on data and algorithms specific to its function.
- **Examples**:
  - Virtual assistants like Siri, Alexa, and Google Assistant.
  - Recommendation systems used by Netflix, Amazon, and Spotify.
  - AI-powered spam filters and fraud detection systems.
- **Applications**: Healthcare (diagnosis), customer service (chatbots), manufacturing (robotics), and more.

2. General AI (Strong AI)

- **Definition**: General AI refers to systems with the capability to understand, learn, and apply intelligence across a broad range of tasks, comparable to human cognitive abilities.
- **Characteristics**:
  - Possesses reasoning, problem-solving, and decision-making skills.
  - Capable of learning from experience and transferring knowledge across domains.
  - Demonstrates self-awareness and the ability to adapt to new situations.
- **Current Status**:
  - General AI remains theoretical and is not yet realized.
  - Research is ongoing, with challenges in replicating human-like cognition and understanding.
- **Potential Implications**:
  - Could revolutionize fields like education, healthcare, and research.
  - Raises ethical and safety concerns due to its potential unpredictability.

3. Super AI

- **Definition**: Super AI refers to a hypothetical future AI system that surpasses human intelligence across all fields, including creativity, problem-solving, and emotional intelligence.
- **Characteristics**:
  - Far exceeds human cognitive capabilities in every domain.
  - May develop its own goals and reasoning processes beyond human control or comprehension.

    - Capable of independent innovation and decision-making at an unprecedented scale.
- **Current Status**:
    - Super AI exists only in theoretical discussions and speculative scenarios.
    - Researchers and ethicists debate its feasibility and the potential risks it could pose.
- **Potential Implications**:
    - Could lead to groundbreaking advancements in science, technology, and society.
    - Raises concerns about existential risks, such as loss of human control or unintended consequences.

Key Differences Between the Types

Aspect	Narrow AI	General AI	Super AI
Scope	Task-specific	Multi-domain, general	Beyond human capabilities
Learning Ability	Predefined algorithms	Learns and adapts	Autonomous, self-driven
Current Status	Widely implemented	Theoretical, in progress	Hypothetical

Chapter II: How AI Works

I. Data as the foundation of AI

Data serves as the backbone of artificial intelligence, enabling machines to learn, adapt, and perform tasks. Here's an exploration of how data forms the foundation of AI:

1. The Role of Data in AI

- **Training AI Models**: AI systems, particularly those based on machine learning, rely on large datasets to learn patterns, relationships, and rules.
- **Decision-Making**: Data provides the input for AI to make informed decisions, predictions, or classifications.
- **Feedback and Improvement**: Continuous data collection allows AI systems to refine their performance over time.

2. Types of Data Used in AI

- **Structured Data**: Organized information such as spreadsheets or databases, including numerical values, dates, and categories.
- **Unstructured Data**: Raw data like text, images, audio, and video that require advanced processing to extract insights.
- **Big Data**: Massive datasets collected from various sources, including IoT devices, social media, and transactional systems.

3. The Data Lifecycle in AI Development

- **Data Collection**: Gathering data from sensors, user interactions, databases, or external sources.
- **Data Cleaning**: Ensuring the data is accurate, complete, and free of inconsistencies.
- **Data Labeling**: Annotating data for supervised learning, where the model is trained using labeled examples.
- **Data Storage**: Storing data securely and in a format suitable for processing, often using cloud storage or specialized databases.

4. Key Data Considerations for AI

- **Quality Over Quantity**: High-quality, relevant data is essential for accurate model training.
- **Diversity**: Diverse datasets prevent biases in AI decision-making and ensure broader applicability.
- **Privacy and Security**: Compliance with regulations like GDPR ensures data is handled ethically and securely.

5. Real-World Examples of Data in AI

- **Healthcare**: Patient records, diagnostic images, and treatment outcomes enable AI to assist in medical diagnosis.
- **E-Commerce**: Purchase histories, search data, and customer reviews are used to personalize recommendations.
- **Transportation**: Traffic data and GPS inputs help optimize navigation systems.

II. Machine Learning and Deep Learning explained

Machine learning (ML) and deep learning (DL) are subsets of artificial intelligence, each with distinct methodologies and applications. Here's a breakdown of their concepts, differences, and real-world uses:

1. Machine Learning (ML)

Definition

Machine learning is a subset of AI that enables systems to learn patterns and make decisions without being explicitly programmed. It relies on algorithms trained using data to perform specific tasks.

How It Works

- **Training**: ML algorithms learn from data by identifying patterns and relationships.
- **Testing**: The model is evaluated on new data to measure its performance.
- **Prediction**: After training, the model predicts outcomes based on input data.

Types of Machine Learning

1. **Supervised Learning**:
    - Trained on labeled data (e.g., input-output pairs).
    - Examples: Predicting house prices, email spam detection.

2. **Unsupervised Learning**:
   - Deals with unlabeled data to find patterns or groupings.
   - Examples: Customer segmentation, anomaly detection.
3. **Reinforcement Learning**:
   - The model learns by interacting with an environment, receiving rewards or penalties.
   - Examples: Game-playing AI, robotics.

Applications

- Fraud detection in banking.
- Predictive maintenance in manufacturing.
- Recommendation systems (e.g., Netflix, Amazon).

---

2. Deep Learning (DL)

Definition

Deep learning is a specialized subset of ML that uses neural networks with multiple layers (hence "deep") to process and learn from large volumes of data.

How It Works

- **Neural Networks**: Mimic the structure of the human brain, consisting of interconnected layers of nodes (neurons).
- **Feature Extraction**: Unlike traditional ML, deep learning automatically extracts relevant features from raw data, reducing the need for manual intervention.

Key Components

1. **Input Layer**: Receives raw data (e.g., images, text).
2. **Hidden Layers**: Perform computations to extract features and patterns.
3. **Output Layer**: Produces predictions or classifications.

Popular Architectures

- **Convolutional Neural Networks (CNNs)**: Excel in image recognition tasks.
- **Recurrent Neural Networks (RNNs)**: Handle sequential data like time series or text.
- **Transformers**: Power language models like GPT for natural language processing.

Applications

- Image and facial recognition.
- Language translation and chatbots.
- Autonomous vehicles (e.g., Tesla's Autopilot).

3. Key Differences Between Machine Learning and Deep Learning

Aspect	Machine Learning	Deep Learning
Data Dependency	Performs well with smaller datasets.	Requires large amounts of data to perform well.
Feature Engineering	Requires manual feature extraction by	Automatically extracts features from raw

Aspect	Machine Learning	Deep Learning
	experts.	data.
Complexity	Simpler algorithms like decision trees, SVMs.	Uses complex architectures like neural networks.
Computation Power	Requires less computational power.	Needs high-performance GPUs and TPUs.
Training Time	Faster training times.	Longer training times due to complexity.

4. When to Use ML vs. DL

- **Machine Learning**: Ideal for smaller datasets, structured data, or when interpretability is critical.
    - Example: Predicting stock prices using historical data.
- **Deep Learning**: Suited for large datasets, complex problems, and unstructured data like images and text.
    - Example: Identifying objects in real-time video feeds.

III. Neural Networks: The Building Blocks of AI Systems

Neural networks are at the heart of modern AI systems, enabling machines to process and interpret complex data. Inspired by the structure and functioning of the human brain, they are used to solve a wide range of problems, from image recognition to natural language processing.

1. What Are Neural Networks?

A neural network is a computational model designed to recognize patterns and relationships within data. It consists of layers of interconnected nodes (or neurons), where each node processes input data and passes the results to the next layer.

2. Structure of a Neural Network

Layers

1. **Input Layer**:
    - Receives raw data (e.g., pixels in an image, numerical values).
    - Passes this data to the subsequent layers for processing.
2. **Hidden Layers**:
    - Perform the actual computations to extract features and patterns.

        - The depth (number of layers) and width (number of neurons per layer) determine the network's complexity.
   3. **Output Layer**:
        - Produces the final result, such as a prediction or classification.

Neurons and Weights

- **Neurons**: Each neuron processes incoming data using a mathematical function.
- **Weights**: Assigned to connections between neurons, weights determine the importance of each input.
- **Bias**: Adjusts the output of the neuron to better fit the model to the data.

---

3. How Neural Networks Learn

Forward Propagation

- Data flows through the network from the input layer to the output layer.
- Each neuron applies an activation function to its input, determining its output.

Loss Function

- Measures the difference between the predicted output and the actual value (error).

Backpropagation

- The error is propagated backward through the network to adjust the weights and biases.

- This process minimizes the error by iteratively updating the network parameters using optimization techniques like gradient descent.

4. Types of Neural Networks

1. **Feedforward Neural Networks (FNNs):**
   - Data flows in one direction from input to output.
   - Commonly used for simple tasks like classification and regression.
2. **Convolutional Neural Networks (CNNs):**
   - Specialized for processing image data.
   - Uses convolutional layers to extract spatial features (e.g., edges, shapes).
3. **Recurrent Neural Networks (RNNs):**
   - Designed for sequential data like time series or text.
   - Incorporates memory of past inputs to handle temporal dependencies.
4. **Generative Adversarial Networks (GANs):**
   - Consists of two networks (generator and discriminator) that compete to create realistic data.
   - Used in applications like image synthesis and deepfake generation.
5. **Transformers**:
   - Revolutionized natural language processing by capturing contextual relationships in text.
   - Power large language models like GPT and BERT.

5. Applications of Neural Networks

- **Healthcare**: Diagnosing diseases from medical images (e.g., X-rays, MRIs).
- **Finance**: Predicting stock prices and detecting fraudulent transactions.
- **Retail**: Personalizing shopping experiences through recommendation systems.
- **Entertainment**: Enhancing gaming experiences and creating virtual worlds.
- **Autonomous Vehicles**: Processing sensor data for real-time decision-making.

6. Challenges and Limitations

- **Data Requirements**: Neural networks require large amounts of labeled data to perform effectively.
- **Computational Power**: Training deep networks demands significant processing resources.
- **Interpretability**: Complex models can be difficult to understand and explain (black-box nature).
- **Overfitting**: Networks may perform well on training data but fail to generalize to new inputs.

Chapter III: Future Trends in AI
I. The Breakthroughs Shaping Tomorrow

Artificial Intelligence is evolving at an unprecedented pace, with groundbreaking advancements set to redefine industries and everyday life. Below are the most significant trends and innovations shaping the future of AI:

1. General AI (Artificial General Intelligence)

- **What It Is**: AI capable of understanding, learning, and applying intelligence across diverse tasks, much like a human.
- **Potential Impact**:
    - Revolutionize problem-solving and creativity.
    - Enable machines to perform any intellectual task a human can do.
- **Challenges**: Ethical concerns, computational complexity, and the need for massive datasets.

2. AI and Quantum Computing

- **What It Is**: Combining AI with quantum computing to process information at exponentially faster speeds.
- **Potential Impact**:
    - Solve problems currently beyond the reach of classical computers, such as complex simulations in physics and biology.
    - Enhance machine learning by optimizing algorithms and accelerating training processes.

- **Current Progress**: Companies like IBM, Google, and startups are making strides in quantum-AI integration.

3. Neurosymbolic AI

- **What It Is**: A hybrid approach combining symbolic reasoning (logic-based AI) with neural networks (data-driven AI).
- **Potential Impact**:
    - More interpretable AI systems that reason and learn simultaneously.
    - Applications in fields requiring a blend of structured logic and data-driven insights, like legal tech or medical diagnostics.

4. Edge AI

- **What It Is**: AI computation performed directly on devices (e.g., smartphones, IoT devices) rather than centralized servers.
- **Potential Impact**:
    - Enhanced privacy, as data remains on the device.
    - Reduced latency and faster response times for real-time applications.
- **Applications**: Smart home devices, wearable health monitors, autonomous drones.

5. AI in Healthcare

- **Breakthrough Areas**:
    - **Personalized Medicine**: AI analyzes genetic and lifestyle data to recommend tailored treatments.
    - **Drug Discovery**: Accelerating the development of new drugs using AI-powered simulations.
    - **Robotic Surgery**: Improving precision and reducing recovery times.
- **Future Implications**: A paradigm shift in diagnostics, treatment planning, and patient care.

6. AI and Creativity

- **Generative AI**: Tools like DALL·E, GPT, and others are pushing the boundaries of creativity in art, writing, and design.
- **Future Possibilities**:
    - Co-creating films, music, and literature with human artists.
    - AI architects and designers shaping buildings and products.

7. Ethical and Responsible AI

- **Focus Areas**:
    - Developing transparent and interpretable AI systems to ensure accountability.
    - Mitigating biases to create fairer AI solutions.
    - Establishing global regulations for safe and ethical AI deployment.
- **Impact**: Building trust and societal acceptance of AI technologies.

8. AI for Sustainability

- **Applications**:
    - Optimizing energy use in smart cities.
    - Monitoring and predicting climate patterns.
    - Reducing waste in supply chains through AI-driven logistics.
- **Future Implications**: Accelerating progress toward global sustainability goals.

9. Human-AI Collaboration

- **What It Is**: Enhancing human abilities with AI rather than replacing them.
- **Future Trends**:
    - Augmented intelligence systems that empower professionals in fields like education, law, and medicine.
    - AI assistants that act as lifelong learning partners or productivity enhancers.

10. Autonomous Systems

- **Advances in Robotics and Automation**:
    - Self-driving cars and delivery drones becoming more reliable and mainstream.
    - Advanced robotics in manufacturing and service industries.

Chapter III: Future Trends in AI

I. The Breakthroughs Shaping Tomorrow

Artificial intelligence is at the forefront of technological innovation, with breakthroughs that promise to transform industries, enhance human capabilities, and address global challenges. Here's a look at the major advancements shaping the future of AI:

1. Artificial General Intelligence (AGI)

- **What It Is**: The development of AI systems capable of performing any intellectual task that a human can do, with the ability to generalize knowledge across different domains.
- **Potential Impact**:
  - Revolutionize problem-solving, creativity, and decision-making.
  - Enable AI to assist in complex, multidisciplinary challenges like climate change or space exploration.
- **Current Status**: While AGI remains a long-term goal, advances in multitask learning and reasoning systems are bringing us closer.

2. Quantum AI

- **What It Is**: Integration of quantum computing with AI to solve problems that are currently computationally infeasible.

- **Potential Impact**:
    - Accelerate machine learning training and optimization.
    - Solve complex simulations in fields like chemistry, logistics, and cryptography.
- **Key Players**: Google, IBM, and other tech giants are making strides in combining AI with quantum technologies.

3. Neurosymbolic AI

- **What It Is**: A hybrid approach that combines neural networks with symbolic reasoning to enhance learning and interpretability.
- **Potential Impact**:
    - Make AI systems more transparent and explainable.
    - Excel in domains requiring both logical reasoning and pattern recognition, such as healthcare and legal systems.

4. Transformative AI Models

- **Breakthrough Technologies**: Large language models like GPT, BERT, and multimodal models (e.g., OpenAI's DALL·E) are pushing the boundaries of creativity and problem-solving.
- **Potential Impact**:
    - Seamless human-AI collaboration in content creation, education, and personalized assistance.

- Real-time language translation and global communication improvements.

5. Edge AI and Federated Learning

- **What It Is**: AI computation performed on local devices rather than centralized servers, often using decentralized data training methods.
- **Potential Impact**:
  - Enhanced privacy and reduced latency in AI applications.
  - Democratization of AI technology, making it accessible in areas with limited connectivity.
- **Applications**: Smart home devices, wearable technology, and autonomous vehicles.

6. AI-Driven Drug Discovery and Precision Medicine

- **What It Is**: Using AI to simulate biological processes and identify potential drug candidates faster.
- **Potential Impact**:
  - Drastically reduce the time and cost of drug development.
  - Enable personalized treatments based on an individual's genetic and lifestyle data.
- **Key Achievements**: AI has already identified promising drug candidates for conditions like Alzheimer's and cancer.

7. Generative AI and Creativity

- **Breakthroughs**: Generative models are advancing the creation of text, images, music, and videos.
- **Potential Impact**:
    - Revolutionize creative industries, from filmmaking to gaming.
    - Enable co-creation between humans and AI for art, design, and architecture.
- **Challenges**: Ethical concerns, such as copyright issues and misuse of deepfakes.

8. AI in Climate and Environmental Sustainability

- **Applications**:
    - Predicting and mitigating climate change through advanced modeling.
    - Enhancing renewable energy systems with optimized efficiency.
    - Monitoring deforestation, wildlife patterns, and pollution using AI-powered drones and sensors.
- **Potential Impact**: AI could accelerate progress toward global sustainability goals, preserving ecosystems and combating resource depletion.

9. Autonomous Systems and Robotics

- **Advances**: Improvements in AI-driven robotics, from self-driving cars to advanced manufacturing robots.
- **Potential Impact**:
  - Streamline supply chains and logistics.
  - Enhance productivity in sectors like agriculture and construction.
  - Introduce smart assistants and caregivers for aging populations.

10. Ethical and Inclusive AI

- **What It Is**: Developing AI systems that are fair, transparent, and inclusive.
- **Potential Impact**:
  - Minimize biases in decision-making systems.
  - Build trust in AI applications across diverse communities.
- **Current Efforts**: Collaboration between governments, academia, and the private sector to establish global AI ethics standards.

II. Key industries disrupted by AI advancements

Artificial intelligence is at the forefront of technological innovation, with breakthroughs that promise to transform industries, enhance human capabilities, and address global challenges. Here's a look at the major advancements shaping the future of AI:

1. Artificial General Intelligence (AGI)

- **What It Is**: The development of AI systems capable of performing any intellectual task that a human can do, with the ability to generalize knowledge across different domains.
- **Potential Impact**:
    - Revolutionize problem-solving, creativity, and decision-making.
    - Enable AI to assist in complex, multidisciplinary challenges like climate change or space exploration.
- **Current Status**: While AGI remains a long-term goal, advances in multitask learning and reasoning systems are bringing us closer.

2. Quantum AI

- **What It Is**: Integration of quantum computing with AI to solve problems that are currently computationally infeasible.
- **Potential Impact**:
    - Accelerate machine learning training and optimization.
    - Solve complex simulations in fields like chemistry, logistics, and cryptography.
- **Key Players**: Google, IBM, and other tech giants are making strides in combining AI with quantum technologies.

3. Neurosymbolic AI

- **What It Is**: A hybrid approach that combines neural networks with symbolic reasoning to enhance learning and interpretability.
- **Potential Impact**:
    - Make AI systems more transparent and explainable.
    - Excel in domains requiring both logical reasoning and pattern recognition, such as healthcare and legal systems.

4. Transformative AI Models

- **Breakthrough Technologies**: Large language models like GPT, BERT, and multimodal models (e.g., OpenAI's DALL·E) are pushing the boundaries of creativity and problem-solving.
- **Potential Impact**:
    - Seamless human-AI collaboration in content creation, education, and personalized assistance.
    - Real-time language translation and global communication improvements.

5. Edge AI and Federated Learning

- **What It Is**: AI computation performed on local devices rather than centralized servers, often using decentralized data training methods.
- **Potential Impact**:
    - Enhanced privacy and reduced latency in AI applications.

- - Democratization of AI technology, making it accessible in areas with limited connectivity.
  - **Applications**: Smart home devices, wearable technology, and autonomous vehicles.

6. AI-Driven Drug Discovery and Precision Medicine

- **What It Is**: Using AI to simulate biological processes and identify potential drug candidates faster.
- **Potential Impact**:
  - Drastically reduce the time and cost of drug development.
  - Enable personalized treatments based on an individual's genetic and lifestyle data.
- **Key Achievements**: AI has already identified promising drug candidates for conditions like Alzheimer's and cancer.

7. Generative AI and Creativity

- **Breakthroughs**: Generative models are advancing the creation of text, images, music, and videos.
- **Potential Impact**:
  - Revolutionize creative industries, from filmmaking to gaming.
  - Enable co-creation between humans and AI for art, design, and architecture.
- **Challenges**: Ethical concerns, such as copyright issues and misuse of deepfakes.

8. AI in Climate and Environmental Sustainability

- **Applications**:
    - Predicting and mitigating climate change through advanced modeling.
    - Enhancing renewable energy systems with optimized efficiency.
    - Monitoring deforestation, wildlife patterns, and pollution using AI-powered drones and sensors.
- **Potential Impact**: AI could accelerate progress toward global sustainability goals, preserving ecosystems and combating resource depletion.

9. Autonomous Systems and Robotics

- **Advances**: Improvements in AI-driven robotics, from self-driving cars to advanced manufacturing robots.
- **Potential Impact**:
    - Streamline supply chains and logistics.
    - Enhance productivity in sectors like agriculture and construction.
    - Introduce smart assistants and caregivers for aging populations.

10. Ethical and Inclusive AI

- **What It Is**: Developing AI systems that are fair, transparent, and inclusive.
- **Potential Impact**:
  - Minimize biases in decision-making systems.
  - Build trust in AI applications across diverse communities.
- **Current Efforts**: Collaboration between governments, academia, and the private sector to establish global AI ethics standards.

Chapter IV: AI in the Workplace

I. Streamlining workflows with AI automation

Artificial intelligence is transforming workplace productivity by automating repetitive tasks, optimizing processes, and enhancing decision-making. AI-driven automation helps organizations reduce operational costs, improve efficiency, and enable employees to focus on higher-value tasks.

1. How AI Automation Enhances Workflows

1.1 Task Automation

- **Repetitive Tasks**: AI automates mundane, repetitive tasks such as data entry, scheduling, and report generation.
- **Examples**:
    - **Human Resources**: Automating resume screening and onboarding workflows.
    - **Accounting**: AI tools like expense tracking and automated invoicing.

1.2 Process Optimization

- **Workflow Analysis**: AI analyzes existing processes to identify inefficiencies and bottlenecks.
- **Dynamic Resource Allocation**: Intelligent systems adapt resource allocation based on workload predictions.
- **Examples**: AI optimizing supply chain management in logistics and inventory planning.

1.3 Intelligent Assistance

- **AI Assistants**: Tools like virtual assistants (e.g., chatbots) streamline employee interactions with systems, reducing response times.
- **Examples**:
    - Scheduling meetings with tools like Microsoft's Cortana or Google Assistant.
    - Real-time transcription of meetings using AI-powered software like Otter.ai.

2. Applications Across Workplace Functions

2.1 Communication and Collaboration

- AI facilitates collaboration by automating meeting summaries, translating communications, and prioritizing emails.
- Tools like Slack and Zoom integrate AI to enhance workplace connectivity.

2.2 Decision-Making Support

- AI analyzes data patterns to provide actionable insights, empowering leaders to make informed decisions.
- Example: AI-powered dashboards for real-time performance monitoring in sales and marketing.

2.3 Customer Support and Interaction

- AI chatbots handle customer queries 24/7, improving response times and reducing workloads on human teams.

- Example: Automated customer service platforms like Zendesk and Intercom.

2.4 Predictive Maintenance

- In industries like manufacturing, AI monitors equipment in real time to predict and prevent breakdowns.
- Benefits include reduced downtime and extended machinery lifespan.

3. Benefits of AI Automation in the Workplace

3.1 Increased Efficiency

- Automating routine tasks allows employees to focus on creative and strategic activities.

3.2 Cost Reduction

- By reducing manual labor and errors, AI automation helps lower operational expenses.

3.3 Improved Accuracy

- AI minimizes human errors in data processing and decision-making.

3.4 Scalability

- Businesses can scale operations efficiently as AI systems handle increased workloads.

4. Challenges of AI Automation in Workflows

4.1 Workforce Adaptation

- Employees need to reskill to adapt to AI-driven tools and workflows.

4.2 Integration Issues

- Implementing AI systems requires aligning them with existing processes and infrastructure.

4.3 Ethical and Security Concerns

- Ensuring data privacy and mitigating bias in automated decision-making systems are critical challenges.

II. Tools like ChatGPT, Notion AI, and their applications

AI-powered tools such as ChatGPT and Notion AI are redefining productivity and creativity by providing innovative solutions for various professional and personal tasks. These tools leverage advanced natural language processing (NLP) and machine learning to assist users in generating, organizing, and optimizing content efficiently.

1. ChatGPT

Overview

ChatGPT is an advanced conversational AI developed by OpenAI. It uses the GPT architecture to understand and generate human-like text across a wide range of topics.

Applications

1. **Content Creation**:
    - Writing articles, essays, or reports.
    - Crafting social media posts, captions, and ad copy.
    - Generating ideas for creative writing, such as stories or scripts.
2. **Customer Support**:
    - Automating responses to common customer inquiries.
    - Serving as a virtual assistant for businesses, available 24/7.
3. **Education and Learning**:
    - Explaining complex concepts in simple terms.

- Assisting with homework, coding, or language learning.
4. **Brainstorming and Ideation**:
    - Providing suggestions for projects, business strategies, or research topics.
5. **Personal Assistance**:
    - Drafting professional emails and resumes.
    - Organizing to-do lists or scheduling activities.

2. Notion AI

Overview

Notion AI is an extension of the Notion workspace, a tool designed for organization and collaboration. Notion AI integrates artificial intelligence to help users streamline note-taking, project management, and content creation.

Applications

1. **Writing and Summarizing**:
    - Generating first drafts of articles, meeting notes, and project updates.
    - Summarizing lengthy documents or research materials.
2. **Task Management**:
    - Automating task descriptions and reminders in project workflows.
    - Providing action items based on meeting notes or brainstorming sessions.
3. **Knowledge Management**:
    - Organizing information into structured formats for easy reference.

- Creating databases with AI-assisted categorization and tagging.
4. **Collaboration**:
    - Assisting teams by providing content templates and suggestions.
    - Streamlining communication with shared AI-generated summaries.

3. Key Differences and Complementary Features

Aspect	ChatGPT	Notion AI
Primary Function	Conversational AI for text generation and problem-solving.	Productivity and organization with AI-driven assistance.
Use Case	General-purpose writing, brainstorming, and Q&A.	Project management, content organization, and team collaboration.
Integration	Standalone or via APIs for custom applications.	Embedded within Notion's workspace for seamless integration.

4. Combined Use Cases

1. **Content Workflow**:
    - Use ChatGPT for brainstorming and generating content ideas.
    - Organize and refine these ideas using Notion AI's collaborative tools.
2. **Team Productivity**:

- Employ Notion AI to manage projects and document progress.
- Use ChatGPT for generating quick replies, presentations, or strategic plans.
3. **Education and Research**:
   - ChatGPT explains concepts or assists with writing papers.
   - Notion AI structures research data and provides summarized insights.

5. Benefits of These Tools

1. **Efficiency**: Accelerate tasks like writing, brainstorming, and organizing.
2. **Cost-Effectiveness**: Reduce dependency on human resources for repetitive tasks.
3. **Accessibility**: Provide easy-to-use interfaces for users of all skill levels.
4. **Customization**: Adapt to various workflows, industries, and personal needs.

Chapter V: AI and Creativity

I. AI in Writing, Art, and Music

Artificial intelligence is reshaping the creative landscape, pushing the boundaries of imagination and productivity in writing, art, and music. By augmenting human creativity with computational power, AI has enabled novel forms of expression while streamlining traditional creative processes.

1. AI in Writing

AI-powered tools are transforming how we create and consume written content, making the process faster and more accessible.

Applications:

1. **Content Generation**:
   - Platforms like ChatGPT and Jasper AI assist in drafting articles, blogs, essays, and scripts.
   - Authors use AI for generating story ideas, character development, or plot twists.
2. **Editing and Proofreading**:
   - AI tools like Grammarly and ProWritingAid help refine grammar, style, and tone.
   - They ensure clarity and consistency in professional documents and creative works.
3. **Interactive Storytelling**:
   - AI-driven narrative platforms create immersive choose-your-own-adventure experiences.

- Examples include AI Dungeon, which lets users collaborate with AI to build dynamic stories.

Impact on Writing:

- Enhances productivity for writers, journalists, and marketers.
- Democratizes content creation, allowing non-experts to craft compelling pieces.
- Raises ethical questions about originality and authorship.

2. AI in Art

AI tools are revolutionizing visual art by offering new methods for creating, analyzing, and appreciating art.

Applications:

1. **Generative Art**:
   - Tools like DALL·E and MidJourney generate unique images from text prompts.
   - Artists use AI to produce visuals that blend diverse styles and concepts.
2. **Restoration and Enhancement**:
   - AI restores damaged artworks, preserving cultural heritage.
   - It enhances resolution and colorizes old photographs or videos.
3. **Augmented Creativity**:
   - Artists collaborate with AI to explore styles beyond traditional human capabilities.
   - AI-powered apps like DeepArt apply famous artistic styles to photographs.

Impact on Art:

- Expands the definition and accessibility of art creation.
- Challenges traditional notions of authorship and creativity.
- Raises intellectual property concerns in generated art.

3. AI in Music

AI has made music creation more intuitive and accessible, enabling amateurs and professionals to innovate.

Applications:

1. **Composition and Production**:
   - Tools like AIVA and Amper Music compose original music tailored to specific moods or genres.
   - AI assists in generating melodies, harmonies, and beats.
2. **Music Recommendation**:
   - Algorithms like those used by Spotify and Pandora analyze user preferences to curate playlists.
3. **Performance and Remixing**:
   - AI recreates music in the style of iconic artists or remixes existing tracks.
   - Tools help identify and remove vocals or instruments for mashups or karaoke.
4. **Music Restoration and Analysis**:
   - AI enhances old recordings and identifies patterns or themes in music history.

Impact on Music:

- Makes composition accessible to non-musicians.
- Enables faster, iterative creative processes for professionals.
- Raises questions about emotional authenticity in AI-composed music.

4. Benefits of AI in Creativity

- **Efficiency**: Speeds up creative workflows by automating repetitive tasks.
- **Accessibility**: Opens doors for amateurs to explore creative pursuits.
- **Innovation**: Encourages blending of styles and techniques, creating entirely new genres.

5. Challenges and Concerns

- **Authenticity**: Concerns about whether AI-generated works have emotional depth or cultural significance.
- **Ethics and Ownership**: Determining authorship and protecting intellectual property rights.
- **Dependence on AI**: Risk of diminishing human creativity and over-reliance on automated systems.

II. Leveraging AI to Enhance Creative Processes

AI has become a powerful tool for enhancing creativity across various fields. By automating repetitive tasks, offering new ideas, and providing advanced analytics, AI is transforming how artists, writers, musicians, and designers create and innovate. Here's a look at how AI can be leveraged to enhance creative processes:

1. Idea Generation and Brainstorming

AI can be an excellent partner in the early stages of the creative process, helping individuals and teams overcome creative blocks and generate new ideas quickly.

How It Works:

- **AI-Driven Inspiration**: Tools like ChatGPT and Jasper can help generate creative ideas based on a given prompt, offering suggestions for stories, artwork, or design concepts.
- **Randomization for Creativity**: AI algorithms can mix different styles, genres, or formats to create new, unexpected results.
- **Collaborative Creativity**: Platforms like AI Dungeon allow for collaborative storytelling with AI, where users can interact with the AI to create dynamic narratives.

Example:

A novelist might use ChatGPT to brainstorm plot ideas or character names, while an artist could prompt an AI tool like DALL·E to create concept art for a new visual project.

2. Enhancing Design and Visual Arts

AI tools in the design and visual arts domains can elevate creativity by introducing new techniques, styles, and possibilities for expression.

How It Works:

- **Generative Art**: AI algorithms can generate unique artwork based on user input, providing endless variations of a theme. Tools like DALL·E and DeepArt use neural networks to create visually compelling art.
- **Style Transfer**: AI can transform images by applying famous art styles, such as turning a photograph into a painting in the style of Van Gogh or Picasso.
- **Image Editing and Enhancement**: AI tools like Adobe Sensei and Prisma offer intelligent editing features such as auto-color correction, background removal, or upscaling, allowing artists to focus on the creative aspect of their work.

Example:

A graphic designer could use AI to create an array of logo designs, quickly iterating on concepts without needing to manually draw every variation.

3. AI in Music Composition and Production

AI has revolutionized music composition, enabling musicians to create complex compositions with minimal effort while exploring new musical territories.

How It Works:

- **AI Composition**: Tools like AIVA (Artificial Intelligence Virtual Artist) and Amper Music use AI to generate original music based on parameters such as mood, genre, and tempo.
- **Music Collaboration**: Musicians can collaborate with AI to experiment with different sounds, harmonies, or instruments, expanding their creative horizons.
- **AI Remixing and Sound Design**: AI tools can remix existing tracks or produce unique sound effects that can be incorporated into new compositions.

Example:

A composer working on a film score might use AI to generate multiple variations of a theme, experimenting with different instruments and tempos to see which resonates best with the mood of the scene.

4. Writing and Storytelling

AI can streamline the writing process by offering tools that generate content, assist in drafting, and provide linguistic enhancements.

How It Works:

- **Content Generation**: AI tools like ChatGPT and Copy.ai can help generate first drafts, outline ideas, or provide alternative wording, allowing writers to focus on refining ideas rather than starting from scratch.

- **Story Plotting and Character Development**: AI can assist in developing story arcs, character backstories, and dialogue, enhancing the narrative-building process.
- **Editing and Proofreading**: AI-based writing assistants such as Grammarly or ProWritingAid suggest grammar improvements, style adjustments, and readability enhancements, allowing writers to focus on creativity while ensuring their work is polished.

Example:

A screenwriter could use AI to generate dialogue suggestions for characters, helping to overcome writer's block and add diversity to conversations.

5. Creative Collaboration Between Humans and AI

AI doesn't replace human creativity; rather, it serves as a powerful partner in the creative process, offering assistance and inspiration while allowing the human creator to retain control over the final product.

How It Works:

- **Co-Creation**: Artists, writers, and musicians can use AI as a collaborative tool, where the AI suggests, generates, or modifies ideas, and the creator refines and personalizes the output.
- **Idea Refinement**: AI can help refine and improve ideas by analyzing patterns, audience preferences, or feedback from previous work to generate relevant, high-impact results.

- **Cross-Domain Collaboration**: Creatives in different fields (e.g., a designer and a musician) can work together, leveraging AI tools to generate cohesive, multidisciplinary projects.

Example:

A filmmaker could collaborate with AI tools for both visual effects (using AI-generated art) and music composition (using AI-generated soundtracks) to create an immersive cinematic experience.

6. AI-Powered Feedback and Optimization

AI can also be used to refine and optimize creative projects based on feedback, audience reactions, and data analysis.

How It Works:

- **Audience Analysis**: AI tools analyze audience reactions to creative works—such as social media sentiment analysis or viewer engagement with videos—to suggest improvements in content creation.
- **Performance Optimization**: AI tools predict how well creative pieces will perform in specific contexts, adjusting elements such as timing, color schemes, or storytelling techniques to maximize impact.
- **A/B Testing**: AI can run experiments and analyze different versions of creative content (e.g., headlines, images, or music) to determine which is most effective for a particular audience.

Example:

A marketer could use AI to analyze which social media posts resonate best with audiences, adjusting the messaging or visuals based on the feedback.

---

7. Personalization and Customization

AI enables personalized creative experiences, allowing for highly tailored content creation based on individual preferences, behaviors, or demographics.

How It Works:

- **Targeted Content Creation**: AI can help creators produce customized content, from personalized advertisements to user-specific recommendations in art, music, and writing.
- **Interactive Creativity**: AI enables the creation of personalized interactive experiences, such as custom playlists, art pieces, or narrative experiences that adapt to the user's choices.

Example:

A digital artist may use AI to generate personalized art based on a viewer's preferences, or a musician may create adaptive soundtracks that change depending on a listener's mood.

Chapter VI: AI in Education

I. Personalized Learning with AI Tools

AI is transforming education by enabling personalized learning experiences that cater to the unique needs, preferences, and abilities of each student. With AI tools, educators can provide tailored learning paths, real-time feedback, and more engaging content, making education more effective and accessible for all learners.

1. What is Personalized Learning?

Personalized learning refers to an educational approach where the pace, content, and learning strategies are customized to meet the individual needs and preferences of each student. AI enhances personalized learning by analyzing student data and adapting the curriculum accordingly.

2. How AI Enables Personalized Learning

2.1 Adaptive Learning Platforms

- **AI-powered platforms** like DreamBox, Knewton, and Squirrel AI adjust the difficulty level of lessons and provide real-time feedback based on the learner's performance.
- **How It Works**: These platforms track a student's progress, identify areas of strength and weakness, and

modify the learning content in real time to match the student's pace and level of understanding.
- **Benefits**: This ensures that students receive targeted help in areas they struggle with while skipping content they already grasp, leading to a more efficient and effective learning process.

2.2 Intelligent Tutoring Systems

- AI-powered **virtual tutors** provide personalized support, answering questions and offering guidance tailored to individual learning needs.
- **How It Works**: These systems use natural language processing (NLP) to understand student queries and provide explanations. For example, platforms like Carnegie Learning and Coursera's AI assistants offer one-on-one help in subjects like math, science, and languages.
- **Benefits**: Students can receive 24/7 help, working through problems and concepts at their own pace, without waiting for human instructors.

2.3 Learning Analytics and Insights

- AI tools analyze student data to uncover patterns and provide actionable insights to educators and students.
- **How It Works**: Learning management systems (LMS) like Canvas and Blackboard integrate AI to track engagement, participation, and assessment performance, allowing educators to intervene early when students are struggling.
- **Benefits**: This proactive approach helps identify at-risk students, enabling timely interventions to prevent failure and improve learning outcomes.

3. AI Tools for Personalized Learning

3.1 AI-Powered Educational Apps

- **Applications**: Tools like **Quizlet** and **Duolingo** use AI to adjust the difficulty of exercises and lessons based on a user's progress. For example, Duolingo's language-learning app adapts lessons to the user's proficiency level, providing custom review sessions when needed.
- **Benefits**: Students receive personalized practice and reinforcement, ensuring that they master new skills before moving on to more advanced concepts.

3.2 Virtual and Augmented Reality (VR/AR)

- **How AI Works with VR/AR**: AI-powered VR and AR tools can create immersive, interactive learning environments that adapt to the learner's responses. For example, AI can track a student's interactions within a virtual science lab or history simulation, offering custom challenges or explanations based on their progress.
- **Applications**: Tools like **ClassVR** use VR headsets and AI to offer personalized lessons in subjects like anatomy, history, and geography, enhancing student engagement and understanding.

3.3 AI-Driven Content Creation

- **How It Works**: AI tools can generate personalized learning materials, such as quizzes, flashcards, and study guides, based on the student's current curriculum and learning needs.
- **Applications**: Tools like **Kahoot!** and **Quizlet** use AI to tailor content based on student performance, allowing teachers to create interactive activities that cater to each student's level and learning style.

- **Benefits**: Teachers can provide differentiated content that aligns with each student's unique needs, making lessons more engaging and effective.

4. Benefits of AI-Driven Personalized Learning

4.1 Tailored Instruction

- AI allows teachers to provide instruction that meets individual students' learning styles, speeds, and preferences, creating a more customized and effective educational experience.
- **Example**: A student who excels in math may receive more challenging problems, while a student who struggles with reading might receive additional vocabulary exercises.

4.2 Immediate Feedback

- AI enables students to receive instant feedback on assignments, quizzes, and activities, allowing them to understand their mistakes and improve without delay.
- **Example**: In math, AI tools can automatically assess a student's work, provide corrections, and suggest further practice materials tailored to their weaknesses.

4.3 Learning at Own Pace

- AI-powered systems allow students to learn at their own pace, reducing the pressure of keeping up with a fixed class schedule and enabling mastery of concepts before moving on to the next topic.

- **Example**: Adaptive platforms let students spend extra time on difficult subjects while allowing them to skip ahead in areas they find easy or already know.

4.4 Increased Student Engagement

- By customizing the learning experience, AI can make lessons more engaging, relevant, and enjoyable, which improves student motivation and participation.
- **Example**: Interactive simulations or AI-driven games make learning fun, encouraging students to stay engaged and take ownership of their educational journey.

5. Challenges and Considerations

5.1 Data Privacy and Security

- The use of AI in education requires careful handling of student data. Schools and educators must ensure that personal information is protected and that AI systems comply with data privacy regulations like GDPR.

5.2 Equity and Accessibility

- Not all students have equal access to the technology required for AI-powered learning tools. It's important to ensure that AI enhances educational equity and doesn't exacerbate digital divides between students of different socio-economic backgrounds.

5.3 Teacher Role and AI Integration

- While AI provides powerful tools for personalized learning, it's essential that teachers remain involved in guiding, mentoring, and interpreting the insights generated by AI systems. The teacher's role as a human facilitator and support system cannot be replaced by AI.

II. Transforming education systems through AI integration

AI is revolutionizing education systems across the globe, not just through personalized learning, but by transforming how institutions manage operations, deliver content, and support both students and teachers. By integrating AI at various levels, education systems can become more efficient, inclusive, and adaptive, improving overall outcomes for learners and educators alike.

1. AI in Curriculum and Content Development

AI is transforming how educational content is created, tailored, and delivered, allowing for highly dynamic and responsive curriculums.

How AI Works in Curriculum Development:

- **Adaptive Learning Systems**: AI analyzes vast amounts of data from student interactions to understand where learners are struggling and where they excel, providing insights into how curricula can be adjusted.
- **Automated Content Creation**: AI tools can assist teachers and content developers in creating custom learning materials, such as lesson plans, assessments, and exercises, based on student needs and learning progress.
- **Continuous Updates**: AI helps educators stay updated with the latest advancements in educational content, automatically incorporating new findings, topics, or methodologies into lesson materials.

Benefits:

- Ensures that the curriculum is always aligned with the most current knowledge and standards.
- Provides customized content, ensuring every student can access lessons tailored to their learning style and pace.

2. Intelligent Classroom Management

AI is revolutionizing classroom management, improving organization, communication, and overall classroom dynamics, making it easier for teachers to focus on instruction.

How AI Works in Classroom Management:

- **Attendance and Behavior Monitoring**: AI systems, powered by facial recognition or voice analysis, can track student attendance and even monitor classroom behavior, alerting educators to potential disruptions or challenges.
- **Real-time Student Engagement**: AI can monitor student engagement and participation through analysis of responses, interactions, or even body language, providing immediate insights to teachers about who needs more attention or support.
- **Learning Analytics**: AI systems can collect data from a variety of sources, including student assessments, engagement levels, and feedback, offering teachers a comprehensive overview of classroom performance.

Benefits:

- Streamlines administrative tasks, allowing educators to focus on teaching.
- Provides teachers with real-time insights on student progress and engagement, enabling timely interventions.
- Improves classroom dynamics by identifying and addressing behavioral or engagement issues early.

3. AI for Administrative Efficiency

The integration of AI in educational administration has the potential to significantly improve operational efficiency, reducing administrative burdens and optimizing resource allocation.

How AI Works in Administration:

- **Automating Administrative Tasks**: AI can automate routine administrative tasks such as grading, scheduling, and handling student queries, allowing educators and staff to spend more time on strategic and pedagogical activities.
- **Predictive Analytics for Resource Allocation**: AI analyzes historical data to predict future trends in student enrollment, course demand, and teacher workload, helping institutions allocate resources more effectively.
- **Student Support Systems**: AI chatbots and virtual assistants can provide 24/7 support to students, answering questions about assignments, deadlines, and campus services.

Benefits:

- Reduces time spent on repetitive tasks, increasing productivity among faculty and administrative staff.
- Improves operational efficiency by optimizing resource allocation and workload distribution.
- Provides timely, accessible support for students, enhancing their overall educational experience.

---

4. AI in Assessment and Evaluation

AI is transforming how student performance is assessed, moving away from traditional exams and offering more dynamic and comprehensive evaluation methods.

How AI Works in Assessment:

- **Automated Grading**: AI systems can grade assignments, quizzes, and essays quickly and consistently, providing instant feedback to students. This frees up time for educators to focus on more subjective aspects of student evaluation.
- **Formative Assessments**: AI can continuously assess students' understanding in real time, adapting to their performance during lessons and providing feedback and resources as needed.
- **Personalized Evaluation**: AI analyzes a wide range of data (grades, participation, and assessments) to generate a personalized report on each student's strengths and weaknesses, guiding future instruction and learning goals.

Benefits:

- Increases the efficiency of grading and evaluation, making it easier for educators to manage larger class sizes.
- Provides real-time, detailed feedback, helping students improve continuously rather than waiting for final exam results.
- Allows for more holistic and personalized assessment methods, moving beyond traditional testing and focusing on a learner's individual growth.

5. Inclusive Education through AI

AI holds significant promise in making education more inclusive, ensuring that all students, including those with disabilities, can access quality learning experiences.

How AI Promotes Inclusivity:

- **Assistive Technologies**: AI-powered tools like speech-to-text, text-to-speech, and real-time translation can support students with disabilities, such as those with hearing or visual impairments, in accessing content in ways that suit their needs.
- **Language Support**: AI systems can provide real-time translation, enabling students who speak different languages to engage with educational content in their native language.
- **Personalized Learning Paths**: AI tools can identify learning gaps and disabilities, adjusting lesson content to provide personalized support for students with specific needs, ensuring they receive the right level of assistance.

Benefits:

- Ensures that students with disabilities can fully participate in education, removing barriers to learning.
- Promotes diversity in the classroom by catering to students from varied linguistic and cultural backgrounds.
- Fosters an inclusive environment where all students, regardless of their challenges, can thrive.

6. AI-Enhanced Teacher Training and Professional Development

AI is also transforming how educators themselves learn, grow, and develop their skills, ensuring they are better equipped to handle diverse classrooms.

How AI Supports Teacher Development:

- **Personalized Professional Development**: AI tools can assess a teacher's performance, providing feedback on areas for improvement and recommending personalized professional development courses or strategies.
- **Virtual Classrooms for Teacher Practice**: AI-powered virtual environments allow teachers to practice classroom management, lesson delivery, and student interactions in simulated classrooms, gaining experience without the risk of real-world consequences.
- **AI Mentoring**: AI-driven mentoring platforms can pair new educators with experienced teachers and offer personalized coaching based on their needs, helping them grow in their teaching careers.

Benefits:

- Provides teachers with continuous, personalized support for their professional growth.
- Helps new educators gain confidence and experience through simulated environments.
- Improves the quality of education by ensuring that teachers receive the training they need to be effective in diverse and modern classrooms.

7. Ethical Considerations and Challenges in AI Integration

While AI offers numerous benefits for transforming education systems, it is important to address the ethical challenges associated with its use.

Challenges and Concerns:

- **Data Privacy**: AI systems rely heavily on data, raising concerns about student privacy and how data is collected, stored, and used. Ensuring that AI tools comply with data protection regulations like GDPR is critical.
- **Bias in AI**: AI algorithms may inadvertently perpetuate biases present in training data, leading to unfair outcomes in assessments, teacher evaluations, or personalized learning paths.
- **Equity and Access**: There is a risk that AI could widen the digital divide, particularly in underfunded schools or regions with limited access to technology. Ensuring that AI tools are accessible to all students, regardless of socio-economic background, is essential.

Chapter VII: AI for Business Growth

I. Optimizing operations with AI-driven solutions

AI is becoming a cornerstone of operational optimization for businesses, offering solutions that enhance efficiency, reduce costs, and drive innovation. By integrating AI into various aspects of business operations, companies can streamline processes, improve decision-making, and create a competitive edge in the marketplace.

1. Automating Routine Tasks and Processes

One of the most significant ways AI optimizes business operations is through automation, eliminating time-consuming, repetitive tasks that would otherwise require human intervention.

How AI Automates Operations:

- **Robotic Process Automation (RPA)**: AI-driven RPA tools, such as UiPath and Automation Anywhere, automate routine administrative tasks like data entry, invoice processing, and scheduling.
- **Chatbots and Virtual Assistants**: AI-powered chatbots (like Drift and Intercom) handle customer inquiries, process simple transactions, and provide 24/7 customer support without requiring human agents.
- **Supply Chain Automation**: AI systems can predict demand, optimize inventory management, and automate ordering processes, reducing the need for manual oversight and improving efficiency.

Benefits:

- **Cost Savings**: Reduces labor costs by automating tasks that were previously performed manually.
- **Increased Productivity**: Employees are freed up from mundane tasks and can focus on more strategic work.
- **Faster Decision Making**: Automated systems allow businesses to make faster, data-driven decisions in real-time.

2. Improving Decision-Making with AI Analytics

AI is revolutionizing how businesses make decisions by leveraging data analytics to provide deeper insights, predict trends, and optimize strategies.

How AI Enhances Decision-Making:

- **Predictive Analytics**: AI algorithms analyze historical data to forecast future trends, helping businesses predict sales, market conditions, and customer behavior. For example, companies like **Salesforce Einstein** use AI to offer predictive insights into sales pipelines, customer interactions, and marketing effectiveness.
- **Business Intelligence (BI)**: AI-powered BI tools, such as **Power BI** and **Tableau**, allow businesses to visualize data, track KPIs, and make informed decisions. These tools can spot patterns in vast amounts of data that would be difficult for human analysts to detect.
- **Data-Driven Insights**: AI uses machine learning to continuously improve and adapt its decision-making models, ensuring that businesses have access to the most current and accurate information.

Benefits:

- **Enhanced Forecasting**: AI helps businesses anticipate changes in the market, improving the accuracy of financial forecasting and resource allocation.
- **Real-Time Insights**: AI tools provide businesses with real-time data, enabling them to make more informed, timely decisions.
- **Risk Mitigation**: AI's ability to predict potential issues allows businesses to take proactive measures to mitigate risks before they become significant problems.

---

3. Enhancing Customer Experience

AI enhances customer experience by personalizing interactions, improving service quality, and anticipating customer needs, leading to stronger relationships and customer loyalty.

How AI Improves Customer Experience:

- **Personalized Recommendations**: AI systems like **Amazon's recommendation engine** use machine learning to suggest products and services based on a customer's past behavior and preferences. This increases sales and customer satisfaction.
- **Customer Support**: AI-powered chatbots and virtual assistants, such as those used by **Bank of America** (Erica) or **Sephora** (Sephora Virtual Artist), provide immediate, personalized support to customers, answering questions, resolving issues, and guiding users through processes.
- **Sentiment Analysis**: AI tools analyze customer feedback, reviews, and social media conversations to

gauge sentiment and identify areas for improvement. Businesses can quickly address concerns or capitalize on positive feedback.

Benefits:

- **Improved Customer Engagement**: Personalized interactions lead to higher engagement, satisfaction, and retention rates.
- **24/7 Availability**: AI-driven support systems ensure customers receive assistance at any time of day or night, improving service availability.
- **Increased Efficiency**: By automating customer service, businesses can handle more inquiries at once, reducing wait times and operational costs.

4. Optimizing Marketing Strategies

AI allows businesses to enhance their marketing efforts by analyzing consumer behavior, automating campaigns, and optimizing content delivery.

How AI Optimizes Marketing:

- **Targeted Advertising**: AI analyzes consumer data to create highly targeted and personalized advertising campaigns, ensuring that ads are shown to the most relevant audiences. Tools like **Google Ads** and **Facebook Ads** use AI to optimize ad placements based on user preferences, behaviors, and demographics.
- **Content Creation and Optimization**: AI can assist in creating content by suggesting keywords, headlines, and even drafting entire articles. Tools like **Copy.ai** and

Jasper use natural language processing (NLP) to help businesses generate content quickly and efficiently.
- **Email Campaigns**: AI-driven email marketing tools, such as **Mailchimp** and **HubSpot**, use customer data to tailor email content and optimize sending times, increasing the likelihood of engagement.

Benefits:

- **Higher ROI**: AI helps businesses optimize ad spend by targeting the right audience at the right time, leading to a higher return on investment.
- **Increased Conversion Rates**: Personalized content and product recommendations increase the likelihood of conversions.
- **Time and Resource Savings**: Automating marketing tasks frees up time for marketers to focus on strategy and creative tasks.

5. Enhancing Human Resources and Talent Management

AI is transforming how businesses handle recruitment, employee performance, and workforce management, improving efficiency and helping organizations attract and retain top talent.

How AI Supports Human Resources:

- **Recruitment and Talent Acquisition**: AI-powered platforms, like **HireVue** and **Pymetrics**, use machine learning to screen resumes, analyze candidate responses in video interviews, and match the best

candidates with job openings based on skills and experience.
- **Employee Performance**: AI tools can analyze employee performance metrics to identify high performers and those who may need additional support. Tools like **Lattice** provide real-time insights into employee engagement, productivity, and satisfaction.
- **Workforce Optimization**: AI optimizes workforce scheduling and management by analyzing historical data, predicting future staffing needs, and ensuring that the right employees are in the right place at the right time.

Benefits:

- **Better Hiring Decisions**: AI helps HR departments identify the best candidates for the job, reducing bias and improving the overall quality of hires.
- **Improved Employee Retention**: AI tools can help managers identify potential issues before they lead to employee turnover, allowing businesses to take action to retain top talent.
- **Streamlined Processes**: Automating HR tasks like scheduling and performance reviews reduces administrative burden and increases overall efficiency.

6. Supply Chain and Logistics Optimization

AI is reshaping supply chain and logistics operations by improving demand forecasting, optimizing routes, and reducing costs.

How AI Enhances Supply Chain Management:

- **Predictive Demand Forecasting**: AI analyzes historical data, market trends, and other factors to predict demand fluctuations, helping businesses optimize their supply chain and inventory levels.
- **Route Optimization**: AI-powered systems, like those used by **UPS** and **FedEx**, optimize delivery routes in real time, reducing transportation costs and improving delivery times.
- **Inventory Management**: AI tools can predict when stocks will run low and automatically place orders with suppliers, minimizing stockouts and overstocking.

Benefits:

- **Reduced Costs**: AI optimizes routes, inventory, and demand forecasting, leading to significant cost reductions in logistics and supply chain operations.
- **Faster Delivery Times**: Real-time optimizations improve delivery efficiency, helping businesses meet customer expectations for fast shipping.
- **Improved Resource Allocation**: AI helps businesses allocate resources more effectively, ensuring that supplies are available when needed without excess inventory.

II. Revolutionizing Marketing with Personalization and Analytics

AI is transforming the marketing landscape by enabling hyper-personalization and leveraging advanced analytics. Through the use of AI-powered tools and techniques, businesses are able to tailor their marketing strategies to individual customer needs, preferences, and behaviors. This not only enhances customer satisfaction but also boosts business growth by increasing engagement, conversions, and ROI.

1. AI-Powered Personalization

Personalization is one of the most powerful ways AI is revolutionizing marketing. By using data-driven insights, AI allows businesses to create highly personalized experiences for their customers, ensuring that each interaction is relevant, timely, and effective.

How AI Powers Personalization:

- **Customer Segmentation**: AI analyzes vast amounts of customer data to segment audiences based on various factors such as purchasing behavior, interests, demographics, and browsing history. This enables marketers to target highly specific customer groups with tailored messages.
- **Personalized Content**: AI tools like **Dynamic Yield** or **Optimizely** enable businesses to create personalized website content, email campaigns, and advertisements. AI algorithms deliver the most relevant content to individual users, improving engagement rates and conversion potential.
- **Product Recommendations**: AI algorithms, such as those used by **Amazon** or **Netflix**, analyze past behavior and preferences to suggest products or services to customers. This personalized recommendation system enhances the shopping experience and drives sales.

Benefits:

- **Improved Customer Experience**: Personalization makes customers feel understood and valued, fostering stronger relationships and higher satisfaction levels.
- **Increased Conversion Rates**: Personalized marketing messages and product recommendations lead to more relevant offerings, resulting in higher conversion rates.
- **Enhanced Brand Loyalty**: When customers feel that a brand offers products and services suited to their needs, they are more likely to return, increasing customer lifetime value (CLV).

2. AI-Driven Marketing Analytics

AI is fundamentally changing how businesses measure and analyze marketing performance. With advanced analytics, businesses can gain deeper insights into customer behavior, campaign effectiveness, and market trends, leading to better-informed decisions and improved ROI.

How AI Enhances Marketing Analytics:

- **Predictive Analytics**: AI leverages historical data to predict future trends, behaviors, and outcomes. Marketers can use AI to forecast customer buying patterns, seasonal demands, and potential churn, enabling proactive strategies. For instance, AI tools like **Google Analytics** or **HubSpot** provide predictive insights to adjust marketing campaigns in real time.
- **Sentiment Analysis**: AI can analyze customer feedback, social media posts, and online reviews to determine the sentiment toward a brand, product, or service. This

helps businesses understand customer perceptions and fine-tune their marketing strategies.
- **Attribution Modeling**: AI can assess which marketing channels, campaigns, or touchpoints are most effective at converting leads into customers. By accurately attributing conversions, businesses can optimize their marketing budgets and efforts.

Benefits:

- **Informed Decision-Making**: AI analytics provide businesses with valuable insights into customer behavior and campaign performance, allowing marketers to make data-driven decisions.
- **Optimized Marketing Spend**: By understanding which campaigns and channels deliver the best ROI, businesses can allocate marketing budgets more effectively, improving cost-efficiency.
- **Real-Time Optimization**: AI allows for real-time adjustments to marketing campaigns, ensuring that businesses can respond quickly to changing consumer behavior or market conditions.

3. AI-Enhanced Customer Insights

AI is able to process massive amounts of data, providing businesses with a deeper understanding of their customers' needs, motivations, and behaviors.

How AI Uncovers Customer Insights:

- **Behavioral Analysis**: AI can track customer interactions with websites, social media, and apps to analyze their behavior patterns, such as purchase frequency,

browsing habits, and content engagement. This data helps businesses create more targeted marketing campaigns.
- **Customer Journey Mapping**: AI systems track the entire customer journey, from initial awareness to final purchase, providing insights into which touchpoints drive engagement and conversion. This allows marketers to optimize the customer journey for maximum impact.
- **Voice and Image Recognition**: AI tools like **Google Vision** and **IBM Watson** can analyze images and videos, identifying trends in visual content consumption and understanding consumer preferences in a more nuanced way.

Benefits:

- **Deeper Understanding of Customers**: AI enables businesses to gather comprehensive data on customer behavior and preferences, leading to more targeted and effective marketing strategies.
- **Improved Customer Retention**: By understanding what customers want, businesses can deliver more relevant offerings and engage customers in a meaningful way, increasing loyalty and retention.
- **Optimized Customer Journeys**: AI helps identify the most impactful touchpoints in the customer journey, enabling businesses to focus their marketing efforts on areas that drive the most value.

---

4. AI in Social Media Marketing

AI is transforming social media marketing by optimizing content creation, audience targeting, and engagement, making social platforms a more effective marketing channel.

How AI Enhances Social Media Marketing:

- **Automated Content Creation**: AI tools like **Lately.ai** and **Copy.ai** can generate social media posts and captions based on existing content, ensuring consistent and relevant communication with audiences.
- **Audience Targeting**: AI platforms such as **Facebook Ads** or **LinkedIn Ads** use machine learning to help marketers target the most relevant audience segments. AI analyzes user data and interactions to identify the best prospects for a particular campaign.
- **Social Listening and Engagement**: AI tools monitor social media conversations, analyzing customer sentiment and identifying emerging trends. This allows businesses to respond quickly to customer feedback, track brand sentiment, and engage with audiences effectively.

Benefits:

- **Efficient Content Creation**: AI-generated content allows businesses to maintain a consistent social media presence without dedicating excessive time or resources to manual creation.
- **Better Engagement**: By using AI to identify audience segments and trends, businesses can create more engaging and relevant content that resonates with their target market.
- **Real-Time Customer Interaction**: AI-powered tools enable businesses to respond to customer queries, complaints, or feedback in real-time, improving customer service and engagement.

5. AI-Driven Customer Acquisition and Retargeting

AI enhances customer acquisition and retargeting efforts by predicting the most effective strategies for attracting and converting leads.

How AI Supports Acquisition and Retargeting:

- **Lead Scoring and Prediction**: AI analyzes customer data to score leads based on their likelihood to convert. This allows businesses to prioritize high-quality leads and focus efforts on those most likely to result in sales.
- **Dynamic Retargeting**: AI uses machine learning to analyze customer behavior and create dynamic retargeting campaigns that display personalized ads to users who have previously interacted with a business but did not convert.
- **Cross-Channel Campaigns**: AI can manage and optimize campaigns across multiple channels (e.g., email, social media, and search ads), ensuring consistent messaging and improved targeting.

Benefits:

- **Increased Lead Conversion**: AI's ability to prioritize high-quality leads results in a higher conversion rate, reducing the cost of customer acquisition.
- **More Effective Retargeting**: Dynamic retargeting ensures that customers are presented with relevant offers based on their previous interactions, increasing the chances of conversion.
- **Optimized Multi-Channel Campaigns**: AI ensures that marketing messages are consistently delivered across different platforms, reaching customers through the most effective channels.

6. AI for Content Marketing

AI is reshaping content marketing by optimizing content creation, distribution, and performance tracking, helping businesses deliver the right content to the right audience at the right time.

How AI Enhances Content Marketing:

- **Content Optimization**: AI tools like **Grammarly**, **Hemingway Editor**, and **Surfer SEO** help marketers optimize content for readability, SEO, and engagement, ensuring it resonates with audiences.
- **Topic Generation**: AI tools like **BuzzSumo** and **AnswerThePublic** analyze trends and keyword searches to suggest topics that are likely to engage target audiences, helping businesses stay relevant in the ever-changing digital landscape.
- **Content Performance Analysis**: AI-powered tools like **ContentCal** track the performance of content across different platforms and provide insights into what's working and what isn't, allowing for continuous improvement.

Benefits:

- **Improved Content Relevance**: AI helps marketers create content that aligns with audience interests and search behaviors, driving more traffic and engagement.
- **Time Savings**: AI tools automate aspects of content creation and optimization, allowing businesses to produce more high-quality content in less time.
- **Data-Driven Strategy**: AI ensures that content strategies are based on real-time performance data,

allowing businesses to refine and adapt their content marketing efforts quickly.

Chapter VIII: Launching an AI-Powered Business

I. Profitable ideas for AI-based startups

Launching an AI-powered business can be highly lucrative, given the rapid advancements in artificial intelligence and its broad applications across industries. Whether you're focusing on automation, data analysis, or AI-driven services, there are numerous opportunities to capitalize on this transformative technology. Below are some promising and profitable AI-based startup ideas to explore:

1. AI-Powered Personalization Services

Consumers today expect personalized experiences, and businesses are leveraging AI to deliver tailored services and products. Starting an AI-based personalization business can offer significant opportunities across various sectors.

Potential Applications:

- **E-commerce Personalization**: AI-powered recommendation engines can be used to personalize shopping experiences by suggesting products based on user behavior, preferences, and past purchases. Platforms like **Amazon** and **Netflix** already use these strategies to enhance customer engagement and sales.

- **Personalized Marketing**: Using AI, companies can deliver tailored marketing messages, offers, and content to individual customers. For example, AI tools can analyze customer data to send personalized emails or push notifications that resonate with specific demographics or interests.
- **Personalized Learning**: AI can create customized learning experiences in education platforms, adapting the content to suit individual learning styles and paces.

Revenue Model:

- Subscription-based or SaaS (Software as a Service) model for businesses offering AI-powered recommendation or marketing tools.
- Revenue from licensing the technology or providing consulting services.

2. AI-Driven Healthcare Solutions

The healthcare industry is ripe for AI disruption, with AI technologies offering solutions that improve patient care, streamline operations, and optimize treatments.

Potential Applications:

- **AI for Diagnostics**: AI-powered platforms can help doctors identify diseases or conditions through image recognition (e.g., X-rays, MRI scans) or predictive algorithms based on patient data. Companies like **Zebra Medical Vision** and **Aidoc** are already using AI for medical imaging diagnostics.
- **Personalized Treatment Plans**: AI can analyze patient data to provide personalized treatment

recommendations, increasing the effectiveness of treatments.
- **Healthcare Chatbots**: AI-driven chatbots can assist patients by answering medical queries, booking appointments, or providing medication reminders.
- **Health Monitoring**: Wearables and AI systems that monitor health metrics in real time can help patients track conditions like diabetes, heart disease, or mental health.

Revenue Model:

- Subscription model for healthcare providers using AI software.
- Licensing AI models to hospitals, clinics, and health institutions.
- Consulting fees for developing AI-based healthcare solutions.

3. AI-Based Content Creation and Marketing Tools

With the explosion of digital content, businesses are increasingly turning to AI to streamline content creation and marketing efforts. An AI startup focused on content generation or marketing can tap into a growing market.

Potential Applications:

- **Automated Content Writing**: AI tools like **Jasper** and **Copy.ai** help businesses automate the creation of high-quality content, including blog posts, social media updates, and ad copy.

- **AI for Video Production**: AI-driven video editing tools can help businesses create engaging video content with minimal human effort. This can be particularly useful for small businesses and influencers who need professional-quality videos on a budget.
- **Social Media Automation**: AI-powered social media management tools can schedule posts, optimize engagement, and analyze social media performance, making it easier for businesses to manage their online presence.
- **SEO Optimization**: AI can enhance search engine optimization by suggesting keywords, optimizing content structure, and providing recommendations for improving search engine rankings.

Revenue Model:

- Subscription-based software as a service (SaaS) model for content creation tools.
- Pay-per-use or tiered pricing for premium features (e.g., more advanced AI capabilities).
- Freemium model with upselling for additional features or integrations.

4. AI-Powered Business Intelligence (BI) Tools

AI-driven business intelligence tools help organizations gather, analyze, and visualize large datasets to make more informed decisions. Offering AI-powered analytics tools can be a highly profitable venture.

Potential Applications:

- **Predictive Analytics**: AI tools that predict trends, customer behavior, or market fluctuations can be valuable for businesses looking to stay ahead of the curve.
- **Data Visualization**: AI can automatically generate data visualizations, helping businesses make sense of complex datasets quickly and accurately.
- **Competitive Analysis**: AI systems can scrape data from competitors and provide insights on their strategies, pricing, and customer sentiment, giving businesses a competitive advantage.
- **Real-Time Analytics**: AI-powered dashboards and reporting tools provide real-time analytics that help businesses monitor their operations, performance, and key metrics at a glance.

Revenue Model:

- SaaS model where businesses pay a monthly or annual subscription fee to access the AI-powered analytics platform.
- Revenue-sharing model for companies that rely on data-driven insights for decision-making.
- Custom consulting fees for implementing and tailoring AI-driven BI solutions.

5. AI for Cybersecurity

As cyber threats continue to evolve, businesses are increasingly turning to AI to help safeguard sensitive data and protect their operations from security breaches. AI can offer innovative solutions for detecting and preventing cyber threats.

Potential Applications:

- **Threat Detection and Response**: AI can analyze network traffic and user behavior to detect anomalous activities and potential cyber threats, such as data breaches, ransomware attacks, and phishing attempts.
- **Automated Incident Response**: AI-powered systems can automatically respond to security incidents by isolating affected systems, blocking malicious traffic, and alerting security teams.
- **Fraud Detection**: AI can help financial institutions detect fraudulent transactions by analyzing patterns in user behavior and flagging suspicious activities in real time.
- **Security Automation**: AI-driven tools can help automate the process of updating firewalls, patches, and antivirus software, reducing human error and enhancing cybersecurity efficiency.

Revenue Model:

- Subscription-based model for businesses using AI-driven security solutions.
- Licensing AI cybersecurity algorithms to companies looking to integrate them into their own systems.
- Consulting and implementation fees for customizing AI-powered security solutions.

6. AI-Based Automation for Small Businesses

Many small businesses struggle to manage repetitive tasks and improve operational efficiency. Offering AI-based automation solutions specifically tailored for small enterprises can be a lucrative business opportunity.

Potential Applications:

- **Inventory Management**: AI can automate inventory tracking, demand forecasting, and order management, reducing the chances of stockouts or overstocking.
- **Customer Relationship Management (CRM)**: AI-powered CRM systems can automatically track customer interactions, send follow-up emails, and generate leads, improving sales efficiency.
- **Appointment Scheduling**: AI scheduling assistants can help small businesses manage appointments, send reminders, and reduce no-show rates.
- **Accounting and Bookkeeping**: AI tools can automate financial tasks like invoicing, tax calculations, and expense tracking, saving small businesses valuable time and resources.

Revenue Model:

- SaaS subscription model for providing automation tools to small businesses.
- Pay-per-use pricing or tiered subscriptions based on the size and complexity of the business.
- Customization and consulting fees for implementing automation solutions tailored to specific industries.

---

7. AI-Powered Customer Service Solutions

Customer service is a critical aspect of any business, and AI-powered solutions can significantly improve response times, reduce costs, and enhance customer satisfaction. Starting a business focused on AI-driven customer support can be highly profitable.

Potential Applications:

- **AI Chatbots**: Build and deploy AI-powered chatbots that can provide real-time customer support, answer questions, and resolve common issues on websites or through messaging platforms.
- **Voice Assistants**: AI-driven voice assistants can help businesses automate phone support, allowing customers to resolve queries without human intervention.
- **Sentiment Analysis**: AI systems can analyze customer feedback and determine customer sentiment, helping businesses tailor their responses and improve customer interactions.
- **Helpdesk Automation**: AI can help automate ticketing systems, route customer queries to the right department, and offer 24/7 support for a better overall customer experience.

Revenue Model:

- SaaS or subscription model for businesses using AI-powered customer service solutions.
- Custom pricing based on the number of users or interactions, with premium support features for larger enterprises.
- Consulting fees for helping businesses implement and integrate AI-driven customer service tools.

II. Finding resources and building partnerships

Building an AI-powered business requires more than just innovative ideas; it also necessitates the right resources, tools, and partnerships to bring those ideas to life. Establishing strong collaborations, securing funding, and leveraging external resources can help scale your AI startup effectively. Below are key strategies to find resources and build valuable partnerships for your AI venture.

---

1. Accessing Funding for AI Startups

Securing funding is often the first hurdle for AI-based startups. Due to the high costs associated with AI development (data acquisition, infrastructure, specialized talent, etc.), it's essential to identify the right funding sources.

Potential Funding Sources:

- **Venture Capital (VC)**: Many venture capital firms specialize in funding technology and AI startups. Look for VC firms that have a proven track record in investing in AI companies. Popular VC firms in the AI space include **Sequoia Capital, Accel,** and **Andreessen Horowitz**.
- **Angel Investors**: Angel investors often fund early-stage startups and are a good option if you're in the initial stages of development. They tend to offer more flexible terms than VCs. Platforms like **AngelList** or **SeedInvest** can connect you with angel investors focused on AI startups.
- **Government Grants and Subsidies**: Many governments provide grants and subsidies to encourage AI

development and innovation. Look for public funding opportunities such as **EU Horizon 2020** or **U.S. Small Business Innovation Research (SBIR)** grants, which support research and development in AI technologies.
- **Crowdfunding**: For AI projects with consumer-facing applications, crowdfunding platforms like **Kickstarter** or **Indiegogo** can be a way to raise initial capital and test market interest.
- **Accelerators and Incubators**: AI-focused startup accelerators can provide funding, mentorship, and resources. Programs like **Y Combinator**, **AI NexusLab**, and **Techstars AI** help AI startups secure seed funding and gain access to a network of experienced mentors and investors.

Tips for Securing Funding:

- **Create a Solid Business Plan**: Investors want to know the potential return on investment, so ensure your business plan includes a clear value proposition, target market, growth potential, and detailed financial projections.
- **Demonstrate Traction**: Showcase any early success, such as user growth, partnerships, or early-stage product validation. Investors are more likely to back a startup with proven traction or a clear path to revenue.
- **Build a Strong AI Team**: Investors often look for teams with expertise in AI, machine learning, data science, and engineering. A strong technical team will give your startup credibility and increase your chances of securing funding.

2. Building a Talented AI Team

AI startups need a skilled team that understands the technical and business challenges of developing AI-based solutions. Assembling the right team is critical to the success of your AI business.

Key Roles in an AI Startup:

- **AI/ML Engineers**: These are the technical experts responsible for building machine learning models, developing algorithms, and applying AI techniques. They will help develop the core AI technologies of your startup.
- **Data Scientists**: Data scientists specialize in data analysis and model creation. They are responsible for cleaning, processing, and interpreting data to develop actionable insights and improve AI models.
- **Product Managers**: Product managers are responsible for defining the vision of your AI product and ensuring it aligns with customer needs. They bridge the gap between the technical team and the customer.
- **Business Development and Sales Experts**: These professionals focus on finding customers, establishing partnerships, and managing the revenue-generating side of the business. They will help expand your customer base and ensure your AI product meets market demand.
- **UX/UI Designers**: A user-friendly interface is key to the success of AI-based products. UX/UI designers ensure that the AI solutions you develop are intuitive and accessible to users.

How to Build Your AI Team:

- **Leverage AI Talent Pools**: Partner with universities, online platforms like **Kaggle**, and AI bootcamps that offer specialized training to recruit top talent.

- **Hire Freelancers or Contractors**: If your budget is limited or you need specific expertise for a short-term project, consider hiring AI experts from platforms like **Upwork**, **Toptal**, or **Freelancer**.
- **Foster a Collaborative Environment**: Building an AI startup requires a blend of technical skills and creative thinking. Foster a culture of collaboration where engineers, data scientists, and business professionals work together to solve complex problems.

3. Finding AI Tools and Resources

Building AI solutions often requires powerful tools, platforms, and infrastructure. Leveraging the right resources can save your startup time and money while accelerating product development.

AI Development Tools and Frameworks:

- **TensorFlow**: An open-source platform for machine learning developed by Google, used for building and training deep learning models.
- **PyTorch**: Another open-source machine learning library, known for its flexibility and ease of use, developed by Facebook's AI Research lab.
- **Keras**: A high-level neural networks API that runs on top of TensorFlow, enabling fast prototyping and easier model development.
- **Scikit-learn**: A popular Python library for machine learning that provides simple and efficient tools for data mining and data analysis.
- **OpenAI's API**: Leverage pre-trained AI models such as **GPT-3** for natural language processing tasks like chatbots, content generation, or summarization.

- **IBM Watson**: IBM's suite of AI tools and services for natural language processing, visual recognition, and machine learning applications.

Cloud Platforms for AI:

- **Amazon Web Services (AWS)**: Offers AI and machine learning services like **SageMaker**, which can help you build, train, and deploy machine learning models.
- **Microsoft Azure AI**: Provides cloud-based tools and APIs for building AI applications, including **Azure Cognitive Services** for vision, speech, language, and decision-making.
- **Google Cloud AI**: Offers machine learning tools, including **Google AI Platform**, for building AI models, training data pipelines, and deploying machine learning applications.

AI Data Resources:

- **Open Datasets**: There are many publicly available datasets for AI research, including those from sources like **Kaggle**, **UCI Machine Learning Repository**, and **Google Dataset Search**.
- **Synthetic Data Generation**: In some cases, generating synthetic data is a viable option when real-world data is unavailable or expensive. Platforms like **Mostly AI** or **DataGen** offer synthetic data generation tools for training AI models.

Hardware Resources:

- **Graphics Processing Units (GPUs)**: AI model training can be resource-intensive. Using cloud-based GPUs from **AWS**, **Google Cloud**, or **NVIDIA** can help your startup access powerful computing resources without heavy upfront investment in hardware.

- **Edge AI Devices**: For AI applications that require real-time processing, such as in IoT or robotics, edge devices like **NVIDIA Jetson** or **Google Coral** offer affordable options for deploying AI at the edge.

4. Building Strategic Partnerships

In the AI industry, partnerships with other companies, research institutions, and key stakeholders can significantly enhance your startup's capabilities and market reach.

Types of Partnerships:

- **Corporate Partnerships**: Partnering with established businesses can help you access resources, expertise, and customer bases. For instance, collaborating with large tech companies like **Google**, **Microsoft**, or **IBM** can give your AI startup credibility, technical resources, and market access.
- **University Collaborations**: Many universities have AI research labs that work on cutting-edge technologies. Establishing partnerships with universities can provide access to research, talent, and pilot projects.
- **Industry Alliances**: Joining industry-specific organizations like the **Partnership on AI** or **AI Global** allows startups to stay ahead of AI trends and collaborate on regulatory and ethical matters.
- **AI-Enabled Platforms and APIs**: Partnerships with established AI platforms and APIs, such as those offered by **AWS**, **Microsoft**, or **Google**, can help you scale your product offerings without reinventing the wheel.
- **Channel Partnerships**: Partnering with other software companies to integrate your AI technology into their

products can open new distribution channels and accelerate market adoption.

How to Build Effective Partnerships:

- **Align Goals and Values**: Ensure your partners share similar goals and values, especially when it comes to innovation, customer-centricity, and AI ethics.
- **Collaborative Development**: Work with partners to co-develop AI solutions or integrate your technology into their products. Joint product development can help expand your capabilities and reach new customer segments.
- **Networking**: Attend AI and tech conferences like **CES**, **AI Summit**, or **NeurIPS** to meet potential partners, investors, and collaborators. Networking in these events can lead to valuable connections that can help scale your business.

Chapter IX: Managing AI in Organizations

I. Preparing teams for AI adoption

Successfully adopting AI in an organization involves not just acquiring the right tools and technologies, but also preparing teams to effectively integrate AI into their workflows, culture, and operations. Organizational readiness plays a crucial role in maximizing the benefits of AI while minimizing the risks and challenges associated with its implementation. Here are key steps to help prepare teams for AI adoption in an organization:

1. Educate and Upskill Employees

One of the most significant barriers to AI adoption is the knowledge gap. Many employees may have limited exposure to AI, its potential applications, or its implications. Offering comprehensive training and development opportunities can help employees understand AI's capabilities and enhance their ability to work with it.

Steps to Educate and Upskill:

- **Conduct Workshops and Training Sessions**: Organize training sessions for employees at all levels to explain AI concepts, tools, and applications relevant to their roles. For example, product managers could be trained in AI-powered product development tools, while marketing teams learn about AI-driven customer segmentation.
- **Offer Online Courses**: Provide employees with access to online AI courses from platforms like **Coursera**, **edX**, or **Udacity**. Many of these platforms offer beginner to

advanced courses on AI, machine learning, and data science.
- **Bring in AI Experts**: Invite AI consultants or hire internal experts to lead workshops or training sessions that address specific use cases within your industry or business.

Key Areas of Focus:

- **Basic AI Concepts**: Teach the fundamentals of AI, including machine learning, neural networks, and natural language processing, so employees understand how these technologies work.
- **Practical Applications**: Provide real-world examples of how AI can be applied in different business areas (e.g., marketing, customer service, operations) to improve decision-making, efficiency, and customer experience.
- **Ethics and Governance**: Address ethical considerations, including data privacy, bias in AI algorithms, and the responsible use of AI. Train employees on the organization's AI ethics policies and how they should ensure AI is used fairly and transparently.

2. Foster a Culture of Collaboration Between Teams

AI adoption requires cross-functional collaboration. Teams that have traditionally worked in silos need to break down those barriers and work together to make AI a success. AI implementation typically spans across various departments like IT, marketing, data science, operations, and customer service, so fostering collaboration is key.

How to Foster Collaboration:

- **Establish Cross-Functional AI Teams**: Create specialized task forces or committees made up of employees from different departments (e.g., data scientists, engineers, business leaders, and domain experts) to collaborate on AI projects.
- **Encourage Knowledge Sharing**: Implement tools like internal forums, workshops, or knowledge bases where employees from different teams can share their experiences, learnings, and challenges regarding AI initiatives.
- **Involve Non-Technical Teams Early**: Engage business leaders and non-technical teams early in the AI adoption process. Help them understand the potential of AI and how it can solve specific business problems, even if they are not involved in the technical development.

Tips for Successful Collaboration:

- **Set Clear Roles and Expectations**: Clearly define the roles and responsibilities of each team member involved in AI projects. Ensure that all stakeholders understand their contribution to the project's success.
- **Promote Open Communication**: Use collaboration tools like **Slack**, **Trello**, or **Asana** to facilitate communication and task tracking across teams.
- **Encourage a Data-Driven Mindset**: Foster a culture where decision-making is backed by data and AI insights. This mindset should permeate all levels of the organization, from top leadership to operational staff.

3. Align AI Strategy with Business Goals

AI adoption will be more effective if it is directly aligned with the organization's strategic objectives. Teams need to understand how AI fits into the broader vision of the company and how it can help solve business challenges and achieve key performance indicators (KPIs).

Steps to Align AI Strategy:

- **Define Clear AI Goals**: Work with leadership to set specific, measurable goals for AI adoption, such as improving operational efficiency, enhancing customer experience, or increasing revenue.
- **Communicate AI's Value Proposition**: Clearly communicate to teams how AI will help achieve business goals. Show them how AI can improve workflows, reduce manual tasks, and lead to better decision-making.
- **Start with High-Impact Use Cases**: Focus on AI projects that can deliver significant value to the organization in the short term. For example, automating customer service chatbots or implementing AI-powered predictive analytics for sales forecasting. This approach will demonstrate tangible results and help gain buy-in from teams.

How to Ensure Alignment:

- **Leadership Support**: Leadership should actively support and champion AI adoption across the organization. This includes allocating resources, setting expectations, and creating a clear roadmap for AI projects.
- **Regular Progress Reviews**: Establish regular check-ins to monitor the progress of AI initiatives and ensure they are aligned with organizational goals. Adjust the strategy as needed based on feedback from teams and results from AI applications.

4. Encourage Experimentation and Innovation

AI is an evolving field, and employees should be encouraged to experiment and innovate with new AI tools and approaches. A culture that supports experimentation allows teams to explore creative solutions and drive continuous improvement in AI adoption.

Ways to Encourage Experimentation:

- **Create an AI Sandbox**: Offer teams a sandbox or test environment where they can experiment with AI tools, models, and solutions without the pressure of delivering immediate results.
- **Foster an Innovation Mindset**: Reward teams for innovative uses of AI, even if the projects fail. This helps foster a culture where employees feel comfortable taking risks and trying new things.
- **Provide Time for R&D**: Allocate time for teams to explore new AI research, attend conferences, and engage in brainstorming sessions. This will keep the organization up-to-date with AI advancements and open the door to innovative ideas.

Overcoming Barriers to Experimentation:

- **Limitations of Data**: Ensure that employees have access to high-quality, diverse datasets for training and testing AI models. This might require investing in data acquisition or partnerships with data providers.
- **Fear of Change**: Address any concerns about AI replacing jobs by emphasizing how AI will augment human capabilities rather than replace them. AI should

be seen as a tool to help employees be more efficient and focused on higher-value tasks.

5. Implement AI Governance and Ethical Guidelines

As AI adoption grows, it's crucial to implement governance frameworks that ensure AI systems are used ethically, responsibly, and transparently. Employees must be aware of the ethical implications of AI, including bias, fairness, privacy, and accountability.

Steps to Implement AI Governance:

- **Create an AI Ethics Committee**: Establish an AI ethics board to oversee AI projects and ensure they comply with ethical guidelines, data protection regulations, and transparency standards.
- **Develop Clear Guidelines**: Develop company-wide AI ethics policies that outline how AI models are created, tested, and deployed. Include considerations for fairness, data privacy, and transparency.
- **Regular Audits**: Conduct regular audits of AI systems to ensure they are performing as expected and do not introduce bias or unintended consequences.

Ethical Considerations:

- **Data Privacy**: Ensure AI applications comply with data privacy regulations like GDPR (General Data Protection Regulation) and CCPA (California Consumer Privacy Act).
- **Bias in AI**: Train teams to recognize and mitigate bias in AI models by using diverse and representative datasets and ensuring transparency in model development.

- **Human Oversight**: Emphasize the importance of human oversight in AI decisions, especially in sensitive applications like hiring, healthcare, or criminal justice.

II. Navigating challenges and mitigating risks

While AI offers tremendous potential for improving business operations, enhancing decision-making, and driving innovation, its adoption comes with several challenges and risks. Organizations need to anticipate and address these obstacles to ensure AI initiatives are successful and sustainable. Below are common challenges in AI adoption and strategies to mitigate risks associated with these technologies.

---

1. Data Quality and Availability

AI systems rely heavily on data to learn and make decisions. Poor quality, incomplete, or biased data can result in inaccurate or unreliable AI models, leading to suboptimal outcomes.

Challenges:

- **Data Scarcity**: For AI models to be trained effectively, they need large and diverse datasets. In some industries, relevant data may be hard to come by or too expensive to obtain.
- **Data Quality**: AI models are only as good as the data they are trained on. If the data is noisy, incomplete, or outdated, the models may not perform well.
- **Bias in Data**: If the data used to train AI systems is biased, it can lead to biased predictions or decisions,

which may negatively impact outcomes, especially in sensitive areas like hiring, lending, or healthcare.

Mitigation Strategies:

- **Invest in Data Collection and Management**: Prioritize gathering high-quality, diverse datasets that represent the full scope of your problem domain. Establish data governance protocols to ensure that data is accurate, consistent, and up-to-date.
- **Use Synthetic Data**: In cases where real-world data is scarce or sensitive, synthetic data can be generated to train AI models, provided it is representative and accurate.
- **Bias Detection and Correction**: Implement methods to identify and mitigate bias in training datasets. Regularly audit data for bias and ensure diverse representation, especially when the AI is used for decisions that impact people's lives, such as hiring, criminal justice, or healthcare.
- **Data Augmentation**: Use techniques like data augmentation to artificially increase the size and variety of training datasets, improving the model's generalization capability.

2. Lack of Talent and Expertise

AI is a highly specialized field that requires expertise in machine learning, data science, programming, and business strategy. However, skilled professionals in these areas are in high demand and short supply.

Challenges:

- **Talent Shortage**: The demand for AI professionals far exceeds the available talent pool. Organizations may struggle to recruit and retain qualified staff with the required skills.
- **Complexity of AI Development**: Building and maintaining AI systems requires both domain knowledge and technical expertise. Businesses may find it difficult to manage the complexities of AI models, particularly those that require continuous training and improvement.
- **High Costs of Expertise**: Hiring top AI talent can be expensive, especially for smaller organizations with limited budgets.

Mitigation Strategies:

- **Up-skill Existing Employees**: Offer training and development programs for current employees to help them acquire AI-related skills. This can include online courses, workshops, or partnerships with educational institutions.
- **Collaborate with AI Partners**: If your organization lacks in-house expertise, consider partnering with AI service providers, consultants, or universities that specialize in AI research and development. These partnerships can offer access to advanced AI knowledge without the need for extensive hiring.
- **Outsource AI Development**: For smaller businesses or startups, outsourcing AI development to external experts or firms can reduce costs and provide access to specialized knowledge.
- **Create an AI Center of Excellence**: Establish an internal AI center of excellence that brings together technical experts, data scientists, and business leaders to collaborate on AI initiatives. This helps promote

knowledge sharing and creates a centralized point of expertise.

3. Integration with Existing Systems

Integrating AI into legacy systems and workflows can be challenging. Many businesses use outdated infrastructure, and integrating new AI technologies may require significant changes to existing processes, software, and databases.

Challenges:

- **Legacy Systems**: Existing IT infrastructure may not be compatible with modern AI technologies, requiring costly upgrades or complete overhauls.
- **Data Silos**: In large organizations, data may be siloed across different departments or systems, making it difficult to create a unified view necessary for AI models.
- **Resistance to Change**: Employees and managers accustomed to traditional workflows may resist integrating AI into their daily tasks, creating friction in adoption.

Mitigation Strategies:

- **Incremental Integration**: Instead of a complete overhaul, adopt an incremental approach to integrating AI. Start with small, manageable projects that demonstrate AI's potential, then gradually scale as confidence and capabilities grow.
- **Data Centralization**: Implement solutions that integrate data from disparate sources into a centralized platform.

    This could include using cloud-based services or modern data lakes that allow data from various systems to be aggregated for AI modeling.
- **AI as a Service (AIaaS)**: Leverage cloud-based AI services like **Google AI**, **AWS SageMaker**, or **Microsoft Azure AI** that offer pre-built models and APIs, reducing the need for complex integration with existing systems.
- **Change Management**: Employ effective change management strategies to guide employees through the adoption process. Communicate the benefits of AI and train employees on how the technology will improve their work, rather than replace it.

4. AI Transparency and Explainability

AI models, especially deep learning models, are often referred to as "black boxes" because they make decisions or predictions without offering clear explanations of how those decisions were made. This lack of transparency can lead to trust issues and resistance to AI adoption, particularly in sectors like finance, healthcare, and law.

Challenges:

- **Lack of Transparency**: For stakeholders (customers, regulators, and business leaders) to trust AI models, they must understand how decisions are being made. Lack of transparency can undermine trust and lead to skepticism.
- **Regulatory and Ethical Concerns**: In industries like healthcare or finance, AI decision-making must comply with strict regulatory and ethical standards. The inability to explain how an AI system makes decisions could lead to non-compliance or legal liabilities.

Mitigation Strategies:

- **Adopt Explainable AI (XAI)**: Invest in tools and techniques that improve the transparency and explainability of AI models. This includes techniques like decision trees, rule-based systems, or other interpretable models that provide insights into the decision-making process.
- **Model Auditing**: Regularly audit AI models to ensure they are behaving as expected and to identify any biases, errors, or unethical behaviors. This includes using explainability frameworks and techniques like **LIME** (Local Interpretable Model-Agnostic Explanations) or **SHAP** (SHapley Additive exPlanations).
- **Ensure Regulatory Compliance**: Work with legal and compliance teams to ensure AI models meet regulatory standards, especially in industries like finance, healthcare, and insurance. Document model decisions, maintain model audit trails, and ensure that AI systems are designed for accountability.

---

5. Ethical and Social Implications

AI systems can have significant social, ethical, and legal implications, particularly when used in areas that affect people's lives. Concerns include privacy violations, discrimination, job displacement, and algorithmic bias.

Challenges:

- **Bias and Discrimination**: AI models trained on biased data can perpetuate and amplify existing inequalities, leading to unfair treatment of certain groups.

- **Job Displacement**: AI automation may replace certain jobs, raising concerns about job losses and economic inequality.
- **Privacy Concerns**: AI systems that process sensitive personal data may raise privacy concerns, particularly if data is mishandled or used without proper consent.

Mitigation Strategies:

- **Adopt Ethical AI Frameworks**: Develop and adhere to ethical guidelines that govern AI development and deployment. These frameworks should focus on fairness, transparency, accountability, and the minimization of harm.
- **Conduct Impact Assessments**: Perform social and ethical impact assessments for AI initiatives to understand their potential consequences on employees, customers, and society. Use these insights to design responsible AI systems.
- **Diversify Teams**: Build diverse teams to ensure that different perspectives are considered during the AI development process. This helps identify potential biases and avoid creating solutions that may unintentionally harm marginalized groups.
- **Promote AI for Social Good**: Use AI technologies to address societal challenges, such as improving healthcare access, combating climate change, or enhancing education. Prioritize projects that have a positive social impact and mitigate harm.

6. Security Risks and Cyber Threats

AI systems can be vulnerable to attacks that exploit weaknesses in their models, data, or infrastructure. AI models can be manipulated or misled by adversarial attacks, leading to incorrect predictions or malicious behavior.

Challenges:

- **Adversarial Attacks**: Malicious actors can manipulate AI models by feeding them specially crafted inputs, which can cause the system to make incorrect decisions.
- **Data Privacy Violations**: If AI models use personal or sensitive data, they could become targets for data breaches or unauthorized access.

Mitigation Strategies:

- **Strengthen Model Security**: Implement adversarial training techniques to make AI models more robust against attacks. Use techniques like **adversarial examples** and **defensive distillation** to defend against adversarial inputs.
- **Encrypt Data**: Ensure that sensitive data used by AI models is encrypted both at rest and in transit. Implement strong access control mechanisms to protect data privacy.
- **Regular Security Audits**: Conduct regular security audits and vulnerability assessments on AI systems to identify and address potential risks. Use penetration testing and threat modeling to simulate potential attack scenarios and assess system vulnerabilities.

Chapter X: AI in Healthcare

I. AI-powered diagnostics and medical research

- AI in Diagnostics

AI-powered diagnostics focus on enhancing the accuracy, speed, and accessibility of disease detection and treatment planning. From imaging analysis to personalized medicine, AI is transforming how healthcare professionals diagnose and treat patients.

1. Medical Imaging and Pattern Recognition

AI excels in analyzing medical images such as X-rays, MRIs, CT scans, and ultrasounds. Deep learning models, particularly convolutional neural networks (CNNs), can identify abnormalities with a high degree of accuracy.

- **Cancer Detection**: AI tools can detect cancers, such as breast cancer and lung cancer, by analyzing mammograms and CT scans. For instance, Google's DeepMind has developed AI models that outperform human radiologists in breast cancer detection.
- **Retinal Scans**: AI systems like those developed by Moorfields Eye Hospital and Google Health can diagnose diabetic retinopathy and age-related macular degeneration from retinal scans.
- **Cardiology**: AI algorithms analyze echocardiograms and electrocardiograms (ECGs) to detect arrhythmias, heart disease, and other cardiovascular issues.

2. Early Detection of Diseases

AI models can process vast amounts of clinical data to identify subtle patterns that may indicate the early stages of diseases such as Alzheimer's, Parkinson's, and diabetes. Early detection improves outcomes by enabling timely intervention.

- **Predictive Analytics**: AI analyzes patient history, genetics, and biomarkers to predict the likelihood of developing chronic conditions or rare diseases.
- **Symptom Checkers**: Consumer-facing AI tools like Babylon Health or Ada help users assess symptoms and suggest potential conditions, directing them to seek medical care when necessary.

3. Pathology and Genomics

AI can assist pathologists by automating the analysis of tissue samples and identifying markers for diseases such as cancer. In genomics, AI processes genetic data to uncover mutations and variations associated with specific diseases.

- **AI in Pathology**: AI-powered platforms analyze digital pathology slides to classify tumor types, grades, and subtypes, supporting more precise diagnoses.
- **AI in Genomics**: AI algorithms like those from companies like Deep Genomics or Illumina identify disease-linked genetic mutations, aiding in personalized treatment planning.

- AI in Medical Research

AI is accelerating medical research by automating complex processes, analyzing massive datasets, and uncovering new insights that were previously inaccessible to researchers.

1. Drug Discovery and Development

AI is transforming drug discovery, reducing the time and cost required to develop new treatments by identifying promising drug candidates faster than traditional methods.

- **Target Identification**: AI analyzes biological data to identify potential targets for therapeutic intervention.
- **Drug Screening**: Machine learning models predict how different compounds interact with biological systems, narrowing down the most promising candidates for clinical trials.
- **Example**: AI platforms like Insilico Medicine and Atomwise have identified potential drug candidates for diseases such as fibrosis, cancer, and COVID-19.

2. Clinical Trial Optimization

AI enhances clinical trials by improving patient selection, monitoring, and data analysis.

- **Patient Recruitment**: AI algorithms match eligible patients to trials based on their medical history, genetics, and other criteria, improving enrollment rates and trial diversity.
- **Real-Time Monitoring**: Wearable devices integrated with AI provide continuous monitoring of participants, delivering real-time data on treatment effectiveness and side effects.
- **Trial Design**: AI simulates trial outcomes to optimize protocols and reduce costs.

3. Epidemiology and Public Health

AI helps researchers study the spread of diseases and predict future outbreaks, improving public health responses.

- **Disease Surveillance**: AI analyzes data from social media, search engines, and electronic health records to detect disease outbreaks in real time.
- **Pandemic Modeling**: AI models predict the trajectory of infectious diseases, such as COVID-19, guiding public health interventions and resource allocation.

4. AI-Driven Hypothesis Generation

AI tools generate hypotheses by analyzing vast datasets, including scientific literature, clinical trial data, and patient records.

- **Example**: IBM Watson for Drug Discovery scans millions of scientific papers and clinical trial results to suggest new research directions.

- Benefits of AI-Powered Diagnostics and Research

1. **Improved Accuracy**: AI reduces human error, providing consistent and highly accurate results.
2. **Time Efficiency**: Automated processes allow healthcare professionals and researchers to focus on higher-value tasks.
3. **Cost Reduction**: AI decreases the costs of drug development, diagnostics, and treatments by streamlining processes.

4. **Personalized Medicine**: AI enables treatments tailored to individual patients based on their genetic, environmental, and lifestyle data.

- Challenges and Considerations

Despite its potential, AI in diagnostics and research faces challenges:

1. **Data Privacy**: Protecting sensitive patient data is critical in AI-powered healthcare applications.
2. **Bias in AI Models**: Ensuring fairness and reducing bias in training datasets is essential to avoid discriminatory outcomes.
3. **Regulatory Hurdles**: AI systems must comply with strict healthcare regulations, such as FDA approval in the U.S. or CE marking in Europe.
4. **Integration**: Incorporating AI into existing healthcare systems and workflows requires significant effort and investment.

II. The role of AI in transforming patient care

Artificial intelligence (AI) is reshaping patient care by enhancing diagnosis, improving treatment outcomes, and personalizing healthcare delivery. By leveraging data-driven insights and advanced algorithms, AI empowers healthcare providers to deliver more efficient, effective, and patient-centered care.

1. Enhancing Patient Diagnosis and Monitoring

AI plays a vital role in identifying health issues accurately and monitoring patients in real time, significantly improving early intervention and disease management.

- **Wearable Technology**: Devices equipped with AI, such as smartwatches and fitness trackers, monitor vital signs (e.g., heart rate, oxygen levels, sleep patterns) and alert users or healthcare providers to potential health concerns.
- **Remote Monitoring**: AI-powered telehealth platforms enable continuous patient monitoring, reducing hospital visits and ensuring timely care. For instance, AI can analyze data from home-based devices to detect irregular heart rhythms or early signs of diabetes complications.
- **Virtual Health Assistants**: AI chatbots and virtual assistants guide patients through symptom reporting, provide reminders for medications, and offer health tips tailored to their conditions.

2. Personalizing Treatment Plans

AI enables personalized medicine by analyzing a patient's medical history, genetic profile, and lifestyle factors to recommend tailored treatments.

- **Predictive Analytics**: AI predicts how patients might respond to specific medications, helping doctors choose the most effective options while minimizing side effects.
- **Precision Medicine**: AI integrates genetic data with clinical information to design treatment plans for diseases such as cancer, where tailored therapies like immunotherapy depend on genetic markers.
- **Chronic Disease Management**: AI applications provide individualized care plans for managing chronic conditions like diabetes or hypertension, considering patient-specific factors.

3. Improving Clinical Decision-Making

AI supports clinicians in making faster and more accurate decisions by analyzing complex datasets and offering actionable insights.

- **Diagnostic Support**: AI systems like IBM Watson Health analyze vast amounts of medical data, including research papers, patient records, and clinical guidelines, to assist doctors in diagnosing rare or complex conditions.
- **Treatment Recommendations**: AI tools suggest evidence-based treatment options, streamlining decision-making and reducing the burden on healthcare providers.

- **Risk Stratification**: AI models identify high-risk patients who require immediate attention, such as those at risk for sepsis, heart attacks, or strokes.

4. Revolutionizing Surgery with Robotics and AI

AI-powered robotic systems are transforming surgical procedures by enhancing precision, reducing risks, and improving patient outcomes.

- **Robotic-Assisted Surgery**: Systems like the da Vinci Surgical System use AI to guide minimally invasive procedures, ensuring accuracy and faster recovery times.
- **Pre-Surgical Planning**: AI creates 3D models of a patient's anatomy, allowing surgeons to plan complex procedures with greater pr
- **Real-Time Decision Support**: AI provides real-time feedback during surgeries, helping surgeons navigate challenging scenarios.

5. Empowering Patient Engagement and Self-Care

AI fosters greater patient involvement in their healthcare journey, encouraging proactive health management and self-care.

- **Educational Tools**: AI-powered apps and platforms educate patients about their conditions, promoting informed decision-making.

- **Behavioral Nudges**: AI analyzes behavioral data to encourage healthier habits, such as regular exercise, balanced diets, and medication adherence.
- **Mental Health Support**: AI chatbots and apps like Wysa or Woebot provide mental health resources and support, offering accessible care options for patients in need.

6. Streamlining Administrative Tasks in Patient Care

AI optimizes administrative processes, allowing healthcare professionals to focus more on patient care.

- **Appointment Scheduling**: AI automates scheduling, ensuring efficient allocation of time and resources.
- **Electronic Health Records (EHR) Management**: AI tools simplify EHR documentation by transcribing notes and extracting relevant information, reducing clinician burnout.
- **Insurance Processing**: AI streamlines claims processing and pre-authorization requests, speeding up patient access to care.

- Benefits of AI in Patient Care

1. **Improved Access**: AI-driven telehealth and remote monitoring expand access to care for patients in rural or underserved areas.

2. **Enhanced Outcomes**: Early detection and personalized treatment improve patient outcomes and quality of life.
3. **Cost Efficiency**: Streamlined workflows and targeted treatments reduce healthcare costs for providers and patients alike.

- Challenges and Ethical Considerations

1. **Data Privacy**: Safeguarding patient information is essential as AI relies on vast amounts of sensitive health data.
2. **Bias in Algorithms**: Ensuring fairness and inclusivity in AI models is critical to avoid disparities in care.
3. **Patient Trust**: Building trust in AI-powered tools requires transparency and clear communication about their role in care.

Chapter XI: AI and Smart Living

I. Smart Homes, Autonomous Vehicles, and Beyond

- Smart Homes: The AI-Driven Living Space

AI-powered technologies are making homes more intelligent and responsive by automating tasks, optimizing energy use, and enhancing security.

1. Home Automation Systems

AI integrates with smart devices to automate daily routines and manage home systems seamlessly.

- **Voice Assistants**: Platforms like Amazon Alexa, Google Assistant, and Apple's Siri use natural language processing (NLP) to control smart devices, answer questions, and manage schedules.
- **Lighting and Climate Control**: AI systems learn user preferences to adjust lighting, heating, and cooling automatically, ensuring comfort while saving energy.
- **Smart Appliances**: AI-enabled appliances, such as refrigerators, washing machines, and ovens, optimize performance and notify users of maintenance needs.

2. Enhanced Security

AI enhances home security with intelligent surveillance and alert systems.

- **Facial Recognition**: Smart cameras use AI to recognize faces, distinguishing between family members, guests, and potential intruders.

- **Automated Alerts**: AI analyzes security footage in real-time to detect unusual activity and send instant alerts.
- **Smart Locks**: AI-powered locks allow remote control and grant temporary access to guests via mobile apps.

3. Energy Efficiency

AI helps homeowners reduce energy consumption and costs by optimizing resource use.

- **Smart Thermostats**: Devices like Nest and Ecobee analyze patterns to minimize energy usage while maintaining comfort.
- **Energy Monitoring**: AI tools track power usage and suggest ways to reduce waste, such as identifying energy-hungry appliances.

- Autonomous Vehicles: Revolutionizing Transportation

Autonomous vehicles (AVs) are a leading example of AI's transformative potential in mobility, promising safer, more efficient, and accessible transportation systems.

1. AI-Powered Driving

Self-driving cars use AI algorithms, sensors, and cameras to navigate complex environments and make real-time decisions.

- **Computer Vision**: AI processes visual data to identify obstacles, traffic signs, and road conditions.

- **Sensor Fusion**: AI combines data from LIDAR, radar, and GPS to create a comprehensive understanding of the vehicle's surroundings.
- **Predictive Decision-Making**: Machine learning enables AVs to anticipate other drivers' actions and adapt accordingly.

2. Improved Safety

AI in autonomous vehicles reduces human error, a leading cause of accidents.

- **Collision Avoidance**: AI systems detect potential collisions and take corrective actions, such as braking or steering away.
- **Driver Assistance**: Features like lane-keeping, adaptive cruise control, and parking assistance enhance safety even in semi-autonomous vehicles.

3. Sustainability and Accessibility

- **Electric AVs**: Many autonomous vehicles are electric, reducing emissions and supporting greener transportation.
- **Accessibility**: AI-driven vehicles improve mobility for individuals with disabilities or limited access to traditional transport.

- Beyond Homes and Cars: AI in Smart Living

AI extends its impact to broader areas of life, connecting communities and enhancing urban living.

1. Smart Cities

AI helps cities become more efficient, sustainable, and livable by managing infrastructure a

- **Traffic Management**: AI optimizes traffic flow, reducing congestion with real-time adjustments to traffic signals.
- **Waste Management**: AI monitors waste levels and schedules timely collections, improving efficiency and cleanliness.
- **Public Safety**: AI-powered surveillance systems analyze patterns to prevent crime and respond to emergencies more effectively.

2. Personal Assistants and Wearables

AI enhances daily life through devices that promote health, productivity, and convenience.

- **Wearables**: Smartwatches and fitness trackers use AI to monitor physical activity, sleep patterns, and vital signs.
- **AI Personal Assistants**: Tools like Notion AI or Todoist use machine learning to manage schedules, suggest tasks, and provide reminders.

3. Entertainment and Connectivity

AI enriches how we consume media and interact with the digital world.

- **Content Recommendations**: AI platforms like Netflix and Spotify suggest movies, shows, and music based on user preferences.
- **Gaming**: AI creates adaptive, immersive gaming experiences by responding to player behavior.

- Benefits of AI in Smart Living

1. **Convenience**: AI automates routine tasks, saving time and effort.
2. **Safety**: Intelligent systems improve security and reduce risks at home and on the road.
3. **Sustainability**: AI helps conserve resources and supports eco-friendly practices.
4. **Personalization**: AI tailors environments and experiences to individual preferences and needs.

- Challenges and Considerations

1. **Privacy and Security**: Safeguarding personal data from cyber threats is critical in AI-integrated environments.
2. **Cost**: High initial costs of AI-enabled devices and systems may limit accessibility for some users.
3. **Interoperability**: Ensuring seamless integration across devices from different manufacturers remains a challenge.

II. AI's environmental implications

- Positive Environmental Impacts of AI

AI technologies are instrumental in addressing pressing environmental challenges through optimization, monitoring, and innovation.

1. Optimizing Resource Usage

AI enhances the efficient use of natural and industrial resources, minimizing waste and conserving energy.

- **Energy Management**: Smart grids powered by AI predict energy demand and optimize distribution, reducing waste and promoting renewable energy integration.
- **Water Conservation**: AI monitors water usage in agriculture and urban areas, detecting leaks and optimizing irrigation to prevent overuse.
- **Precision Agriculture**: AI analyzes data from sensors, drones, and satellites to optimize planting, watering, and harvesting, reducing resource consumption and increasing yields.

2. Climate Change Mitigation

AI is crucial in efforts to reduce greenhouse gas emissions and combat climate change.

- **Emission Tracking**: AI models monitor and predict carbon emissions, helping organizations and governments meet reduction targets.
- **Renewable Energy Optimization**: AI improves the efficiency of solar and wind energy systems by predicting weather patterns and adjusting output.

- **Reforestation and Carbon Capture**: AI aids in identifying optimal areas for planting trees and enhances carbon capture technologies.

3. Environmental Monitoring

AI systems provide real-time insights into environmental health, helping to protect ecosystems and biodiversity.

- **Wildlife Conservation**: AI analyzes camera traps, acoustic sensors, and satellite images to monitor endangered species and combat poaching.
- **Pollution Detection**: AI-powered sensors detect air, water, and soil pollutants, enabling timely interventions.
- **Disaster Prediction**: AI forecasts natural disasters like hurricanes, floods, and wildfires, allowing for better preparedness and response.

4. Smart Urban Development

AI contributes to building sustainable cities by optimizing infrastructure and reducing environmental footprints.

- **Traffic Management**: AI systems reduce congestion and vehicle emissions through dynamic traffic control.
- **Waste Management**: AI automates waste sorting and optimizes collection routes, promoting recycling and reducing landfill use.
- **Building Energy Efficiency**: AI-powered systems monitor and adjust heating, cooling, and lighting in buildings, conserving energy.

- Challenges and Negative Environmental Impacts of AI

While AI has the potential to advance sustainability, its development and deployment come with environmental costs.

1. High Energy Consumption

AI models, especially large-scale machine learning systems, require significant computational power, contributing to high energy use.

- **Data Centers**: Training and running AI models consume vast amounts of electricity, often sourced from non-renewable energy.
- **Example**: Training large language models like GPT-3 has a substantial carbon footprint due to intensive computational needs.

2. E-Waste Generation

The rapid development and obsolescence of AI hardware contribute to electronic waste.

- **Short Lifespans**: AI-powered devices like IoT sensors and robotics often have limited lifespans, adding to e-waste.
- **Rare Earth Materials**: The production of AI hardware relies on rare earth elements, whose extraction and disposal harm ecosystems.

3. Algorithmic Bias and Misuse

AI systems may unintentionally harm the environment if not designed with sustainability in mind.

- **Unintended Consequences**: AI used for short-term economic gains may prioritize profits over environmental considerations, exacerbating resource depletion.
- **Biased Models**: Lack of environmental data in training datasets may result in suboptimal decisions affecting sustainability goals.

4. Complex Lifecycle Impacts

AI technologies have a lifecycle—from development to deployment and disposal—that can strain resources and ecosystems.

- **Development**: Energy-intensive training processes contribute to greenhouse gas emissions.
- **Operation**: Continuous use of AI systems in smart devices or autonomous vehicles can increase cumulative energy demands.

- Mitigating AI's Environmental Impact

Addressing these challenges requires innovative solutions and sustainable practices in AI development and deployment.

1. **Renewable Energy Integration**: Powering data centers and AI systems with renewable energy sources reduces carbon emissions.
2. **Energy-Efficient Algorithms**: Developing more efficient AI models and hardware minimizes computational requirements.

3. **Lifecycle Design**: Encouraging sustainable design, production, and recycling practices for AI hardware helps reduce e-waste.
4. **Regulation and Policy**: Governments and organizations should implement policies promoting AI's sustainable use and addressing its environmental impact.
5. **Environmental AI Solutions**: Prioritize AI applications that actively contribute to sustainability, such as conservation efforts and green technology development.

Chapter XII: Ethics and Challenges of AI

I. Privacy, Data Security, and Ethical concerns

AI's reliance on large datasets and powerful algorithms introduces significant challenges related to individual rights and ethical accountability.

1. Privacy Concerns

AI systems often depend on vast amounts of personal data, raising issues around how that data is collected, stored, and used.

- **Data Collection**: AI-driven services like social media, smart devices, and surveillance systems collect sensitive user information, sometimes without explicit consent.
- **Behavior Tracking**: AI algorithms analyze user behavior, preferences, and interactions, which can lead to invasive profiling.
- **Lack of Anonymity**: De-anonymization techniques in AI models can reveal identities even from anonymized datasets.

Example: Facial recognition technologies used in public spaces can track individuals without their knowledge, eroding privacy rights.

2. Data Security Challenges

As AI systems store and process sensitive information, they become targets for cyberattacks, posing risks to personal and organizational data.

- **Hacking and Breaches**: Cybercriminals exploit vulnerabilities in AI systems to access private information or manipulate data.
- **Adversarial Attacks**: Malicious actors can feed deceptive inputs into AI models, causing systems to malfunction or make incorrect decisions.
- **Data Ownership**: Unclear policies about who owns and controls the data used by AI systems can lead to misuse or unauthorized sharing.

3. Ethical Concerns in AI Development and Use

Ethical issues arise in AI due to biases in algorithms, lack of transparency, and unintended consequences.

- **Bias and Discrimination**: AI models trained on biased datasets can perpetuate or amplify existing inequalities.
    - **Example**: Hiring algorithms might favor certain demographics if historical data reflects discriminatory practices.
- **Transparency and Accountability**: Many AI systems operate as "black boxes," making it difficult to understand or challenge their decisions.
- **Autonomy and Consent**: AI's ability to make decisions raises ethical questions about human oversight and accountability, particularly in critical areas like healthcare and criminal justice.
- **Misinformation**: AI-powered tools, such as deepfakes or content-generation systems, can spread false information, undermining trust and societal cohesion.

- Balancing Benefits and Risks

To address privacy, security, and ethical challenges, stakeholders must adopt strategies that balance innovation with accountability.

1. **Privacy Safeguards**:
    - Implement robust data protection regulations, such as GDPR or CCPA, to ensure individuals have control over their data.
    - Use privacy-enhancing technologies like differential privacy or federated learning to minimize risks.
2. **Strengthening Security**:
    - Regularly audit AI systems for vulnerabilities and enforce stringent cybersecurity measures.
    - Develop resilient AI models capable of withstanding adversarial attacks.
3. **Ethical Frameworks**:
    - Incorporate fairness and inclusivity in AI model training and testing processes.
    - Encourage transparency through explainable AI, which makes decisions more interpretable and accountable.
    - Promote ethical guidelines, such as the EU's Ethical Guidelines for Trustworthy AI or the IEEE's Global Initiative on Ethics of Autonomous and Intelligent Systems.
4. **Public Awareness and Engagement**:
    - Educate users about how AI systems work, their benefits, and their risks.
    - Include diverse stakeholders, including ethicists, policymakers, and the public, in discussions about AI governance.

II. Balancing Human Roles with AI Capabilities

- The Complementary Nature of Humans and AI

AI and humans excel in different domains, making them complementary rather than competitive.

1. Strengths of AI

AI thrives in areas requiring data processing, pattern recognition, and automation.

- **Speed and Accuracy**: AI can analyze massive datasets and identify patterns much faster and more accurately than humans.
- **Repetitive Tasks**: Automation powered by AI efficiently handles routine and monotonous tasks, freeing humans for more meaningful work.
- **Scalability**: AI can operate continuously, scaling operations beyond what human effort alone could achieve.

2. Strengths of Humans

Humans bring emotional intelligence, ethical judgment, and creativity to the table—qualities that AI cannot replicate.

- **Empathy and Compassion**: Humans excel in understanding emotions and building relationships, crucial in fields like healthcare and counseling.
- **Critical Thinking**: Human judgment is essential for addressing complex ethical dilemmas and making nuanced decisions.
- **Innovation and Creativity**: While AI can assist in generating ideas, humans remain the primary source of original and imaginative thinking.

- Achieving Synergy Between Humans and AI

To maximize benefits, human roles should focus on areas where intuition, ethics, and creativity are vital, while AI handles tasks best suited to automation and data analysis.

1. Human-AI Collaboration

Creating systems that foster collaboration rather than competition ensures that AI enhances human capabilities.

- **Decision Support**: In fields like medicine or finance, AI provides data-driven insights, while humans make final decisions based on context and values.
- **Creative Partnerships**: Tools like generative AI assist artists, writers, and designers in exploring ideas, but humans guide the creative vision.
- **Augmented Workflows**: AI automates time-consuming processes, allowing humans to focus on strategic and innovative tasks.

2. Redefining Roles in the Workforce

Adapting to AI's impact on jobs requires rethinking roles and reskilling workers for emerging opportunities.

- **Upskilling and Reskilling**: Equipping workers with skills to interact with and manage AI systems ensures they remain relevant in AI-driven industries.
- **New Job Creation**: The rise of AI creates demand for roles like AI trainers, ethicists, and system auditors.
- **Focus on Human-Centric Roles**: Emphasizing roles requiring empathy, interpersonal skills, and ethical

oversight preserves the human element in AI-augmented environments.

3. Ethical Oversight and Governance

Human involvement is critical in overseeing AI systems to ensure they align with societal values and ethical principles.

- **Bias Mitigation**: Humans must monitor AI systems for biases in data and decision-making, ensuring fairness and inclusivity.
- **Accountability**: While AI automates processes, humans must remain accountable for outcomes, particularly in high-stakes fields like law enforcement or healthcare.
- **Transparent Communication**: Maintaining open communication about AI's role and limitations fosters trust and informed decision-making.

- Challenges in Balancing Human Roles and AI

1. Job Displacement

As AI automates tasks, some jobs may become obsolete, requiring proactive efforts to retrain and redeploy affected workers.

2. Over-Reliance on AI

Relying excessively on AI can erode critical thinking skills and reduce human engagement in decision-making.

3. Ethical Risks

Without human oversight, AI systems might make decisions that conflict with societal norms or ethical standards.

4. Resistance to Change

Organizations and individuals may resist adopting AI due to fear of the unknown or perceived threats to traditional roles.

- Strategies for Achieving Balance

1. **Education and Awareness**: Promote understanding of AI's capabilities and limitations to empower individuals and organizations.
2. **Policy and Regulation**: Establish guidelines ensuring AI complements rather than replaces human roles, particularly in sensitive areas.
3. **Inclusive Design**: Develop AI systems that prioritize human collaboration and accessibility.
4. **Focus on Lifelong Learning**: Encourage continuous education and adaptability to prepare for evolving roles in an AI-driven world.

Chapter XIII: Learning AI

I. A Roadmap for Beginners

- A Roadmap for Beginners

Learning artificial intelligence (AI) can seem daunting, but with a structured approach and clear milestones, anyone can build a strong foundation. This roadmap outlines the key steps, skills, and resources to help beginners start their AI journey.

- Step 1: Understand the Basics

1. Familiarize Yourself with AI Concepts

Begin by learning the fundamental ideas behind AI, including its purpose, applications, and limitations.

- **Key Topics**: What is AI, machine learning (ML), deep learning (DL), neural networks, and real-world use cases.
- **Resources**:
    - Online articles (e.g., Towards Data Science, AI-focused blogs).
    - Introductory books like *Artificial Intelligence: A Guide to Intelligent Systems* by Michael Negnevitsky.

2. Learn Basic Programming

A strong grasp of programming is essential for implementing AI models.

- **Languages to Learn**: Python is the most popular language for AI due to its simplicity and extensive libraries.
- **Recommended Tools**: Jupyter Notebook, Anaconda, and IDEs like PyCharm or VS Code.
- **Resources**:
    - Python for Beginners (Official Python Tutorials).
    - Courses like *Python for Everybody* on Coursera.

- Step 2: Build a Foundation in Mathematics

Mathematics is the backbone of AI and ML. Focus on key areas:

1. **Linear Algebra**: Vectors, matrices, eigenvalues, and matrix multiplication.
2. **Probability and Statistics**: Basics of probability, Bayes' theorem, and statistical distributions.
3. **Calculus**: Gradients and optimization techniques.
4. **Algorithms**: Sorting, searching, and understanding time complexity.

Resources:

- Books: *Mathematics for Machine Learning* by Marc Peter Deisenroth, A. Aldo Faisal, and Cheng Soon Ong.
- Online courses: Khan Academy, Brilliant.org, or YouTube tutorials.

- Step 3: Dive into Machine Learning

1. Understand ML Concepts

Learn the core principles of machine learning and its three main types: supervised, unsupervised, and reinforcement learning.

- **Topics to Cover**:
    - Regression, classification, clustering, and recommendation systems.
    - Popular algorithms: Decision Trees, k-Nearest Neighbors, Support Vector Machines, and Neural Networks.

2. Practice with Libraries

- **Popular ML Libraries**: Scikit-learn, TensorFlow, PyTorch.
- **Hands-On Projects**: Build models using datasets from Kaggle, UCI Machine Learning Repository, or Google's TensorFlow datasets.

Resources:

- Courses: *Machine Learning by Andrew Ng* on Coursera.
- Platforms: Kaggle for practice and competitions.

- Step 4: Explore Deep Learning

1. Understand Neural Networks

Learn the structure and working of neural networks, including layers, activation functions, and backpropagation.

- **Topics to Cover**:

- Convolutional Neural Networks (CNNs) for image processing.
- Recurrent Neural Networks (RNNs) and Long Short-Term Memory (LSTM) for sequential data.
- Generative Adversarial Networks (GANs) for creative tasks.

2. Practice with Frameworks

Use deep learning libraries like TensorFlow and PyTorch to implement neural networks.

Resources:

- Books: *Deep Learning* by Ian Goodfellow, Yoshua Bengio, and Aaron Courville.
- Courses: *Deep Learning Specialization* by Andrew Ng on Coursera.

- Step 5: Work on Real-World Projects

1. Choose a Domain

Select a domain of interest, such as healthcare, finance, robotics, or natural language processing (NLP).

2. Create Projects

Build AI models to solve real-world problems. Examples include:

- Predicting house prices using regression models.
- Image recognition using CNNs.
- Chatbots using NLP libraries like Hugging Face.

3. Participate in Competitions

Join AI challenges on platforms like Kaggle, DrivenData, or Zindi to test your skills and gain practical experience.

- Step 6: Stay Updated

AI is a rapidly evolving field. Stay informed about the latest research, tools, and advancements.

- **Follow AI Communities**: Join forums like Reddit's r/MachineLearning, AI Stack Exchange, and GitHub repositories.
- **Research Papers**: Read papers from arXiv and Google Scholar to understand cutting-edge developments.
- **Newsletters**: Subscribe to newsletters like *Import AI* or *Deep Learning Weekly*.

- Suggested Roadmap Timeline

Time Period	Focus
1–2 Months	Learn basics of programming and AI concepts.
2–4 Months	Build a foundation in mathematics.
4–8 Months	Dive into ML concepts and practice coding.
8–12 Months	Explore deep learning and advanced topics.
12+ Months	Work on projects, specialize, and stay updated.

II. Recommended platforms and tools for mastering AI

- Learning Platforms

These platforms provide structured courses, tutorials, and resources to build a strong foundation in AI.

1. Online Course Platforms

- **Coursera**:
    - Courses: *Machine Learning* by Andrew Ng, *Deep Learning Specialization*.
    - Features: Offers certifications, flexible deadlines, and content from top universities.
- **edX**:
    - Courses: *AI for Everyone* by Andrew Ng (offered by Stanford), *Data Science and AI* by Microsoft.
    - Features: Access to university-level courses with options for free auditing.
- **Udemy**:
    - Courses: *Python for Data Science and Machine Learning Bootcamp*, *Complete Guide to TensorFlow for Deep Learning with Python*.
    - Features: Affordable one-time purchase, frequent discounts, and lifetime access.
- **DataCamp**:
    - Focuses on Python, R, and data analysis with interactive coding exercises.

2. Interactive Learning Platforms

- **Kaggle**:
    - Features: Free datasets, beginner-friendly tutorials, and competitions.

- Specialization: Hands-on learning and practice in data science and machine learning.
- **Fast.ai**:
    - Course: *Practical Deep Learning for Coders*.
    - Features: Emphasis on simplifying AI concepts, especially deep learning, for non-experts.
- **Google AI**:
    - Courses: *Machine Learning Crash Course*, TensorFlow tutorials.
    - Features: Free learning materials and guides for beginners and advanced users.

- Development Tools and Libraries

AI development requires practical knowledge of programming languages, frameworks, and tools.

1. Programming Languages

- **Python**: The most widely used language for AI, with extensive libraries and community support.
- **R**: Popular for statistical analysis and data visualization in AI.

2. AI Libraries and Frameworks

- **TensorFlow**:
    - Developed by Google, TensorFlow is a versatile library for building and deploying machine learning models.
    - Tools: TensorFlow Hub (pre-trained models), TensorFlow.js (browser-based AI).
- **PyTorch**:

- Developed by Facebook, PyTorch is preferred for research and experimentation due to its flexibility and dynamic computation graphs.
- Features: TorchServe for deploying trained models.
- **Scikit-learn**:
  - Focuses on machine learning algorithms for tasks like classification, regression, and clustering.
  - Beginner-friendly and widely used in ML projects.
- **Keras**:
  - A high-level API for building neural networks, integrated with TensorFlow.
  - Features: Simplifies deep learning model design.
- **Hugging Face**:
  - Specializes in natural language processing (NLP) with easy-to-use pre-trained models.
  - Tools: Transformers library for NLP tasks like text generation, translation, and summarization.

- Platforms for Hands-On Practice

Practical experience is essential for mastering AI. These platforms provide environments to work on real-world projects.

1. Project Platforms

- **GitHub**:
  - Repository hosting for collaborative coding.

- o Features: Access to open-source AI projects and frameworks.
- **Kaggle**:
  - o Competitions: Solve real-world problems for prizes.
  - o Notebooks: Run and share code in a cloud-based environment.
- **Google Colab**:
  - o Features: Free access to GPUs/TPUs for training AI models.
  - o Specialization: Ideal for running Python notebooks without needing local setups.

2. AI Sandbox Tools

- **RunwayML**: AI tools for creative tasks like image generation, video editing, and more.
- **Teachable Machine by Google**: Simplifies creating machine learning models without coding.

- Resources for Staying Updated

Keeping pace with AI advancements is critical. These platforms provide updates, research papers, and community discussions.

- **ArXiv**: Repository for preprints of academic papers on AI and machine learning.
- **Reddit**:
  - o Subreddits: r/MachineLearning, r/ArtificialIntelligence.
  - o Features: Discussions, news, and resources shared by experts and enthusiasts.
- **AI Newsletters**:

- *Deep Learning Weekly.*
- *Import AI.*
- **Podcasts**:
  - *AI Alignment Podcast.*
  - *The TWIML AI Podcast.*

- Hardware Tools for AI Development

AI development, especially deep learning, often requires specialized hardware.

- **GPUs (Graphics Processing Units)**: NVIDIA GPUs (e.g., RTX series) are widely used for training AI models.
- **Cloud Platforms**:
  - **Google Cloud AI**: Offers AI and ML tools with scalable computing resources.
  - **AWS AI Services**: Provides pre-built AI services and infrastructure for training models.
  - **Microsoft Azure AI**: Comprehensive AI tools for enterprise solutions.

Chapter XIV: Using AI in Everyday Life

I. Communicating effectively with AI tools

- Understanding the Capabilities of AI Tools

1. Recognize What AI Can Do

Different AI tools are designed for specific tasks. Familiarizing yourself with their capabilities ensures you use them optimally.

- **Chatbots and Virtual Assistants**: Assist with scheduling, reminders, and answering questions (e.g., ChatGPT, Google Assistant, Siri).
- **Content Creation Tools**: Generate text, art, or music (e.g., Notion AI, DALL·E, Canva Magic Write).
- **Analytical Tools**: Help analyze data, provide insights, and automate workflows (e.g., Tableau, Grammarly, Microsoft Power BI).

2. Understand Limitations

AI tools are not infallible.

- AI might misinterpret vague or poorly framed inputs.
- Complex or niche tasks may require human intervention.

- Best Practices for Effective Communication

1. Craft Clear and Specific Inputs

AI tools respond to the information provided. The clearer your input, the better the output.

- **Be Precise**: Instead of asking, *"Explain this,"* say, *"Explain the concept of neural networks in simple terms."*
- **Provide Context**: For instance, when using a writing tool, specify the tone, audience, and purpose.

2. Use Iterative Refinement

For complex queries or creative outputs, refining and iterating can yield better results.

- Start with a general query, then adjust based on the response.
- For example:
    - **Initial Input**: "Write an article about AI."
    - **Refined Input**: "Write a 500-word article about AI's role in education for a general audience."

3. Leverage Built-In Features

Many AI tools have advanced settings or specialized modes.

- Use "prompt templates" or pre-defined tasks offered by the tool.
- Explore additional functions like summarization, brainstorming, or problem-solving.

- Enhancing Productivity with AI Tools

1. Task Management and Automation

AI-powered virtual assistants can streamline daily routines:

- Scheduling meetings and setting reminders.
- Managing emails and creating to-do lists.

2. Content Generation and Editing

AI tools like ChatGPT and Grammarly can assist in creating polished documents:

- Drafting emails, articles, or reports.
- Enhancing grammar, style, and readability.

3. Learning and Skill Development

AI-powered apps can personalize learning experiences:

- Language learning tools like Duolingo.
- Coding platforms like Codecademy with interactive AI guidance.

- Building Trust and Reliability

1. Cross-Check Information

Always validate outputs, especially for factual or critical tasks.

- Use credible sources to confirm AI-provided information.

2. Provide Feedback

Many tools improve through user feedback. Highlight inaccuracies or suggest improvements to enhance their effectiveness.

II. Enhancing productivity through AI

Artificial intelligence (AI) is revolutionizing the way we work and live, offering solutions to streamline tasks, automate processes, and enhance overall productivity. From personal assistants to intelligent automation systems, AI tools are helping individuals and organizations work smarter, faster, and more efficiently. Here are several ways AI enhances productivity:

1. Automating Repetitive Tasks

AI excels in automating routine and repetitive tasks, allowing individuals and businesses to focus on more creative and strategic activities.

- **Email Filtering and Sorting**: AI tools like Google's Gmail can automatically sort emails into categories (e.g., Primary, Promotions, Social) and flag important ones for quicker access.
- **Data Entry Automation**: AI-powered systems can extract and enter data from documents and spreadsheets into databases, reducing manual errors and saving time.
- **Document Management**: AI tools like Evernote or Notion can organize and categorize notes, documents, and files automatically, making it easier to retrieve information later.

2. Enhancing Communication and Collaboration

AI tools are improving communication and collaboration across teams, both in-person and remotely.

- **Virtual Assistants**: Tools like Google Assistant, Siri, and Alexa help manage tasks such as scheduling meetings, setting reminders, or answering queries.
- **Automated Meeting Scheduling**: AI tools like x.ai or Clara can automate the process of scheduling meetings, finding suitable time slots for all parties.
- **Real-Time Translation**: AI-powered translation tools like Google Translate and Skype Translator facilitate seamless communication across different languages.
- **Collaborative Workspaces**: Platforms like Slack and Microsoft Teams use AI to organize messages, filter important communications, and suggest relevant documents or tasks.

3. Boosting Creativity and Content Creation

AI is transforming content creation in writing, design, music, and other creative fields, enabling faster workflows and inspiring new ideas.

- **Content Generation**: AI writing tools like ChatGPT, Jasper, or Writesonic can generate drafts, suggest ideas, or improve existing content by enhancing language, tone, or structure.
- **Graphic Design Assistance**: AI platforms like Canva and Adobe Sensei can generate designs based on user input, suggesting layouts, color schemes, and typography.

- **Music and Art Creation**: AI tools such as Amper Music and DALL·E allow users to generate music and visual art, reducing time spent on creative processes while offering fresh perspectives.
- **Video Editing**: AI-based tools like Magisto or Adobe Premiere Pro's Sensei AI automate video editing tasks, such as cutting, stabilizing, or adding effects, making video production quicker and easier.

4. Personalizing Learning and Development

AI has the power to tailor educational content to individual learning styles, optimizing skill acquisition and personal growth.

- **Adaptive Learning Platforms**: Tools like Duolingo and Coursera use AI to adjust difficulty levels based on the learner's progress, ensuring content remains engaging and appropriately challenging.
- **AI Tutors and Chatbots**: AI-powered tutors can provide personalized feedback, answer questions, and guide learners through complex concepts, available on-demand.
- **Skill Development**: Platforms like LinkedIn Learning and Skillshare leverage AI to recommend courses that align with the user's current skills and career goals, optimizing professional growth.

5. Streamlining Customer Service

AI-powered customer service solutions help businesses improve response times, enhance satisfaction, and reduce workloads on human agents.

- **Chatbots**: Tools like Intercom, Drift, and Zendesk use AI chatbots to respond to customer inquiries instantly, providing 24/7 support for common questions and issues.
- **Automated Call Centers**: AI-driven call centers can provide accurate information, route calls to the appropriate human agents, and even analyze conversations to improve customer service processes.
- **Sentiment Analysis**: AI tools analyze customer feedback, social media posts, and reviews to determine sentiments and help businesses respond proactively to customer needs.

6. Optimizing Decision-Making

AI can analyze vast amounts of data to provide insights and support decision-making processes, from market research to business strategy.

- **Predictive Analytics**: AI-driven tools like IBM Watson and Salesforce Einstein analyze data to forecast trends, predict customer behavior, and identify business opportunities.
- **Business Intelligence**: AI tools like Tableau and Power BI help businesses analyze large datasets, visualizing trends and making data-driven decisions in real time.
- **Automated Reporting**: AI can automatically generate reports by pulling data from multiple

sources, saving time and ensuring accuracy in business reporting.

7. Improving Time Management

AI tools can help manage and optimize time, leading to better personal productivity and more effective project management.

- **Task Prioritization**: AI-powered to-do list apps like Todoist or Trello use machine learning to suggest priorities, deadlines, and workflows based on your previous tasks and activities.
- **Smart Calendars**: Tools like Google Calendar and Clockwise use AI to optimize your schedule, find time for deep work, and avoid scheduling conflicts.
- **Focus Assist**: AI-driven tools like RescueTime track how you spend your time online and provide insights on productivity patterns, helping you minimize distractions.

8. Enhancing Personalization

AI offers the ability to personalize everything from shopping recommendations to entertainment preferences, creating more enjoyable and efficient experiences.

- **Personalized Shopping**: AI algorithms recommend products based on your past behavior, preferences, and browsing history (e.g., Amazon, Netflix).
- **Content Recommendations**: AI-driven platforms like Spotify and YouTube analyze user preferences

to suggest personalized playlists, videos, and podcasts.
- **Healthcare Personalization**: AI tools like Fitbits and Apple Health analyze health data to provide customized workout routines, diet plans, and health insights.

Chapter XV: Thriving in the AI Era

1. Preparing your mindset for an AI-driven future

1. Preparing Your Mindset for an AI-Driven Future

As artificial intelligence (AI) continues to transform industries, shape daily life, and alter the way we work, having the right mindset is essential for navigating and thriving in this rapidly evolving landscape. Here's how to prepare for an AI-driven future:

2. Embrace a Growth Mindset

The concept of a **growth mindset**, as coined by psychologist Carol Dweck, is crucial when adapting to AI advancements. This mindset involves the belief that abilities and intelligence can be developed over time through dedication and effort. Here's why it matters in the AI era:

- **Continuous Learning**: AI will continue to evolve, so it's essential to remain adaptable and open to learning new technologies and approaches.
- **Resilience**: AI will disrupt many sectors, but with a growth mindset, you can see challenges as opportunities to upskill and innovate.
- **Curiosity**: Cultivate curiosity to explore AI tools, how they work, and their potential applications. The more you understand AI, the better equipped you'll be to use it effectively.

3. Foster Creativity and Critical Thinking

Although AI is powerful, it still lacks human creativity, emotional intelligence, and complex problem-solving skills. In an AI-driven world, your ability to think critically and creatively will be invaluable.

- **Creativity**: AI can handle repetitive tasks, but it thrives when humans guide it with creative insights. Whether in business, art, or innovation, humans still have the edge in creativity.
- **Critical Thinking**: In an age where AI can analyze vast amounts of data, your ability to critically evaluate and interpret those results is key. Being able to question assumptions, analyze AI-generated insights, and make informed decisions will set you apart.
- **Collaboration with AI**: Rather than viewing AI as a competitor, see it as a tool that augments your capabilities. The future will be about human-AI collaboration, where AI handles routine tasks and humans focus on strategic, creative, and complex problem-solving.

4. Build Digital Literacy and Technical Skills

AI is reshaping industries, and being digitally literate is increasingly becoming a must-have skill. However, technical expertise doesn't require mastering complex algorithms; it's about understanding AI's role and knowing how to work with it.

- **Basic AI Knowledge**: Understanding the fundamentals of machine learning, natural language processing, and data analysis will help you engage more effectively with AI tools.
- **Coding and Programming**: While you don't need to be an expert, learning programming languages

like Python and R can be extremely beneficial for working with AI tools.
- **AI Tools and Applications**: Familiarize yourself with tools such as machine learning platforms, cloud-based AI services, and automation software. These tools are often designed to be user-friendly, so even a non-technical background can be an asset.
- **Data Literacy**: AI operates on data. Understanding data management, visualization, and basic statistical principles will help you better interpret AI-driven insights.

5. Cultivate Emotional Intelligence and Soft Skills

AI is great at processing information, but it lacks emotional intelligence (EI)—the ability to recognize, understand, and manage emotions. In an AI-driven future, EI and other soft skills will remain essential.

- **Empathy and Communication**: While AI can assist with customer service, humans still excel in building relationships. Empathy and effective communication will be critical for managing human relationships in the workplace.
- **Leadership and Collaboration**: As AI automates repetitive tasks, leadership will shift toward managing teams, guiding AI-driven decisions, and fostering collaboration among humans and machines.
- **Adaptability**: AI will continue to reshape the workplace and society at large, so being able to adapt to new roles and responsibilities is crucial.

6. Be Proactive in Addressing Ethical and Social Impacts

AI's rapid advancement presents a range of ethical, social, and legal challenges, from data privacy issues to job displacement. Being proactive in understanding these implications and engaging in conversations about them can help you contribute positively to the AI revolution.

- **Ethical AI**: Understand how AI systems are trained, the potential biases in algorithms, and their implications on privacy and fairness. Advocate for responsible AI development that benefits all communities.
- **Social Impact**: AI will likely affect employment in various sectors. Consider how you can contribute to upskilling and reskilling workers displaced by AI, and explore how AI can be leveraged to address social issues.
- **Regulation and Policy**: Stay informed about AI regulations and policies being developed to ensure ethical use, such as transparency in AI decision-making and the implementation of privacy protections.

7. Stay Agile and Open to New Opportunities

The AI landscape is dynamic, and new opportunities are emerging regularly. Staying agile means you're prepared to seize these opportunities, whether they involve new job roles, entrepreneurial ventures, or innovative business models.

- **Entrepreneurial Mindset**: With AI rapidly transforming industries, there's a wealth of opportunities for those willing to explore new business ideas. AI creates possibilities to build smarter products, services, and processes.

- **Job Transformation**: AI won't necessarily eliminate jobs, but it will change the nature of many roles. Embrace the changes and focus on how your skills can complement AI in new ways, whether by managing AI tools, integrating them into your workflow, or training others in their use.
- **Networking and Communities**: Engage with AI communities, attend conferences, or participate in online forums to stay connected to the latest trends and network with like-minded professionals.

8. Prioritize Lifelong Learning

In a world where AI is evolving rapidly, the concept of lifelong learning is more important than ever.

- **Stay Curious**: AI is a field that is constantly changing. Stay informed about the latest advancements, trends, and research.
- **Take Online Courses**: Platforms like Coursera, edX, and LinkedIn Learning offer AI courses that are tailored to different levels of expertise.
- **Certifications and Degrees**: Consider formal education or certification programs in AI, data science, or related fields to deepen your knowledge and skills.

II. Human skills that remain irreplaceable

While AI has made remarkable strides in automating tasks, processing information, and even mimicking human behaviors, there are several human skills that AI cannot easily replicate or replace. These skills are often deeply rooted in human nature and are essential for creativity, emotional connection, and nuanced decision-making. Here are some human skills that are unlikely to be replaced by AI:

1. Creativity and Innovation

AI can assist with creative tasks, such as generating ideas or suggesting designs, but true creativity—coming up with entirely new concepts, thinking outside the box, or innovating in ways that break boundaries—is still uniquely human. Artists, writers, inventors, and entrepreneurs often rely on intuition, personal experiences, and emotions to drive creativity in ways AI cannot replicate.

2. Emotional Intelligence (EQ)

AI lacks the ability to truly understand, interpret, or respond to human emotions in the deep, nuanced way that humans can. Emotional intelligence involves empathy, emotional regulation, and the ability to build meaningful relationships. Whether it's in leadership, customer service, or personal connections, understanding and navigating emotions is an area where humans excel, making this skill irreplaceable by AI.

3. Complex Problem-Solving and Critical Thinking

AI is excellent at processing large datasets and performing tasks based on set algorithms, but when it comes to complex problem-solving—especially in unpredictable or ambiguous situations—humans are still superior. Humans can synthesize diverse perspectives, think abstractly, and apply moral and ethical considerations to decisions, something AI cannot do autonomously.

4. Ethics and Morality

Ethical reasoning is an inherently human skill. While AI can be programmed to follow certain ethical guidelines, it cannot make value-based decisions or understand the moral implications of a situation in the same way humans can. Humans draw on cultural, social, and personal experiences to navigate ethical dilemmas, while AI is limited to the data and rules it has been given.

5. Leadership and Inspiration

AI can assist with tasks like data analysis or performance tracking, but leadership—motivating people, inspiring teams, and navigating organizational challenges—is a uniquely human skill. Great leaders possess vision, empathy, and the ability to connect with others on a personal level. AI cannot provide the emotional connection and influence required to lead effectively.

6. Human Connection and Social Interaction

While AI can simulate conversations and provide responses, it lacks the true human qualities of connection. Building trust, understanding, and rapport with others involves non-verbal cues, empathy, and shared experiences that AI simply cannot replicate. Whether in personal relationships, healthcare, or customer service, genuine human connection is irreplaceable.

7. Intuition and Gut Feeling

Humans often make decisions based on intuition or "gut feeling," particularly when there is incomplete information or ambiguity. This instinctual ability to assess a situation and make quick judgments, especially in high-pressure environments, is difficult for AI to mimic, as it requires understanding of subtle cues and life experience that AI does not have.

8. Adaptability and Flexibility

Humans are incredibly adaptable. We can adjust to new environments, challenges, and changes, often in ways that AI systems cannot. While AI is designed to perform specific tasks, humans can adjust to entirely new roles, take on unexpected challenges, and pivot quickly when necessary. This ability to change directions and think on the fly is a crucial advantage in unpredictable or rapidly changing environments.

9. Cultural Sensitivity and Understanding

Cultural norms, traditions, and values play a significant role in human behavior and interactions. AI lacks the deep cultural understanding that is required to navigate sensitive situations or make decisions that are appropriate in varying social or cultural contexts. Humans can adapt their behavior and communication style based on cultural differences, something that AI may struggle with.

10. Judgment in Uncertainty

Humans excel in making decisions in situations of uncertainty, where data may be incomplete or contradictory. In fields like law, medicine, and politics, human judgment is necessary to weigh competing factors, consider the long-term consequences, and make ethical decisions. AI, by contrast, typically requires clear data and parameters to make decisions.

www.ingramcontent.com/pod-product-compliance
Lightning Source LLC
Chambersburg PA
CBHW071026240526

45469CB00006BD/2113